Left Alone to Learn
(The Break-up Book)

Michael Eli Vineberg

<u>Acknowledgements</u>

This journey's engine was sparked by you, Sara, and for that I am eternally grateful. You are a spectacular human being and it has been my great fortune to have met you in this lifetime.

A few people were essential to my survival and my growth during the time that I wrote this book. Eden, you are a star and I love you to bits. Leah and Daryl, your support and willingness to be there lovingly and generously for me when I most needed it is etched into my heart. Thank you also to my both parents, who have been sources of abundant love.

I am grateful for the work and efforts of Al Turtle, Marcela Soffchi, and Lucina León.

I also want to thank Miguel De La Rosa for his awesome cover design.

And to Emilia, you little shining light, I am totally in love with you and I've just barely gotten to know you.

Table of Contents

Preface

There are certain places in life that are truly painful and are surrounded by terrible suffering. Circumstance places us in great darkness, and we find ourselves cold and frightened and abandoned. My goal with this text is to achieve the remarkable task of being able to accompany another human being within the experience of losing their partner. If I can even manage to do one percent of what I have set out to do here, it will be one of the greatest things that I have done in my life. I want my book to be the pillow that someone can rest upon, to allow their heart to feel pain, and to come in close and have them receive a big, compassionate hug from me. Some of the corners of the human psyche are rife with agonizing despair, and I know from first-hand experience that even the slightest trace of another person connecting within that emptiness makes a world of difference. My quest is to reach out, to stretch myself via language, to extend my heart as far as I possibly can, with the intention of arriving to those who need it most in these scenarios. It is a horrendous thing to be heartbroken. I just want to do whatever I can here and now to ease the passage for the reader and be of service to their heart and their spirit. God bless.

<u>Hello</u>

Most essential human growth comes with pain and is imposed upon us by life itself. We decide if we want to resist or flow.

If you are reading these words, then you are most likely where I am right now. Broken-hearted and feeling alone. Well, at least there are two of us here, right? It may not be a great consolation, but you are going to have to take what you can get here and now. Get used to that for a little while.

Nobody will be able to replace the unique feeling of the space held by your loved one. Nobody. Don't have illusions about that. But that doesn't mean that nothing can fit into that same space. And this is a really important point. The person who is gone right now was being held in a space *inside of you*. You own that space. Not them. Of course it feels wonderful to know that somebody is inside our heart, in our mind, in our spirit. That we breathe them in and out several times a day. Their warmth, the softness of their skin, their voice, their smell.

I get it. I really do. Like I said, we are two of us here.

Human beings are designed for connection. It is essential to our functioning, to our growth. We learn and develop from our interactions with those around us – for better or worse. You may be inclined to go into a deep, dark black hole here and remove yourself from the world. Don't. You may be inclined to seek out alcohol or drugs to try and self-medicate the pain. Don't. You may want to become self-loathing and beat yourself up about how you ended up here, seeking blame from within. Don't. Accountability is perfectly fine, as long as it's healthy and useful.

It hurts. It hurts so very bad. You probably feel like your heart has been ripped out of your chest and laid bare in the cold outside world. It kind of has. You probably are having a hard time eating, waking up, doing much of anything to be honest. That's normal. You are suffering. Learn to accept that. This book isn't about denial, it is about working from within this difficult and painful space.

I am writing this book not just for you, but for me as well. This journey is one that I am taking toward healing, but one that I wish to share because this place is so damn hard to deal with that a little dose of help can surely go a long way for many other people experiencing something similar.

My wife left me. We have been married for two and a half years. We have a baby on the way. Yup, messy. Painful, horrible, torturous, makes me scream and cry kind of messy. I feel as bad as I have ever felt. Ever. No question about it. But this is where I am, and no amount of thoughts will move me from this place.

And that's exactly where we are going to start. You need to be *right here*. Nothing will make the feelings go away. They *aren't supposed to go away*. Not yet at least. They need to be felt, completely. You read that right. The gnawing emptiness inside your chest and belly will go nowhere until you are willing to accept that it is there and *feel it*. This is a perfectly normal reaction to loss and/or abandonment.

The cure is time and willingness on your part to be here – at least for now. It *will* get better. I promise. Maybe not today. Sorry, I know that it sucks to read that previous line, but it is important.

I don't claim to be an expert here. To be honest, if I were an expert on human relations, I am pretty sure that I would not have ended up here in the first place. And that's something important to note here. Don't take this as some sort of gospel. It isn't. These are the ramblings of one man, one human being, who is telling you what he is doing to be able to healthily traverse a particularly ugly part of his life. I'll give you my wisdom and my suggestions, some acquired on my own, some acquired via a therapeutic path, and some learned through dialogues with close friends and family. You try it out. Play trial and error if you want with the ideas and see what fits for you and what is useless to you. Do you have something better to be doing with your time right now? Feeling like a victim instead and feeling bad for yourself? Yeah, definitely not a better choice. Give this a shot.

This is a purification. A life challenge. Believe me when I tell you that how you do here will have a tremendous impact on who you are coming out of this. Also, it will change what you attract to your life in your next chapter. This is an opportunity, a huge one. Take it, live it, work with it. Make yourself be willing to walk with courage and strength here. You *can* do it. Trust me.

Some starting points. Don't chase them. Don't don't don't don't. And don't. They are where they are because that's what felt better for them. If it helps you a bit, consider the possibility that this may not be a permanent arrangement. But for the sake of being honest with yourself, accept that they are gone. Cry. Cry a lot. You may need to lay down and writhe on the ground or on your bed in pain. Do it. Feel the entirety of the pain. Then rest. Repeat as needed. Like I said, this may take some time. If you find yourself spiraling out of control, take a break from the sadness.

Walk, hike, bike, read. Try to stick to stuff that tends to make you feel better. As much as possible, avoid computers and smartphones. Energy suckers generally.

Talk if you need to talk. As much as you need. Friends and family are awesome here. You'll really get to find out who is there for you when things are rough. Don't take it personally if some of them can't do this for you. It takes a very strong and generous person to help another through these dark times. Seek out and find those gems of human beings and lean on them. Use their offers of support and connection. This is not a time to let pride get in the way. To the contrary, drop your guard and let yourself need some help. Like I mentioned earlier, that space inside you is part of you. It is true that you chose to fill it with this very special someone, but now you are going to learn to fill it with other things. Make no mistake, you aren't going to be able to put something there that will replace them and fill the gap. But you will do the next best thing. And the next best thing is infinitely better than just lying there and doing nothing. So much better!

Stick in the Mud

The idea is not to be stuck. You can most definitely lie on your bed and cry your eyes out. In fact, that's a pretty great idea. Because things are moving through you. Allow the emotions to grab hold and shudder their way through your heart.

Learn to care for yourself a bit more. You need it here. If you aren't hungry, be more economical about what you eat. More strategic, basically. Eat fruits, veggies, maybe salads. Try to stay clear of alcohol and caffeine and sugar, but I get it if you insist on having a bit. Just don't binge. And if you do, well then…brush yourself off and walk forward all over again. The closer that you can get to a pure, raw experience of what is inside you and all around you, the better it will be for you. Vices are essentially escape valves, so they do the exact opposite of helping you feel and see what is there to be felt and seen.

Life is all about falling down and getting back up. Here you are on your ass, covered in dirt, miserable, hurting. I know all about it. It is bad, awful, crappy. Light is so scarce that your psyche probably looks like a cave deep in the heart of the earth. That's ok, for now. We are going to take baby steps, not giant leaps. Patience and time. Make friends with patience. Make friends with your pain. Give it room to exist. Allow it in, allow it to break you apart and rip at your heart. This is your moment on the cross. Like I said, purification. It's real and it is rough. Walk intentionally into the fire. And if you can only stick your big toe into the heat and then run away in pain because it burned too much, then so be it. But go back and do it again. Over and over again. Become courageous, even if you need to start in cowardice and walk from there.

I feel raw here. I alternate between thinking that I can handle this and watching myself fall back down. Sometimes I stay down for a bit, allow it to wash over me and engulf me. Then the wave passes and I continue. These feelings, as intense as they are, come in waves. Tsunamis, but waves nevertheless. We are learning how to surf tsunamis. Let's do it together. I could use a friend.

It is essential to be vulnerable here, at least to yourself. If you can be that way in the face of the rest of the world about how you are feeling right now, even better. This is something that I wrote and posted on my Facebook account for all to see recently. I posted it because I was so darn scared to have people know what I felt. It made me feel weak and exposed. I don't expect you to be so gung-ho, just that you get an idea of where I am headed.

"I was talking this morning with someone very close to me about needs. When I dig deep inside, and it is so scary for me to be open and public about this...so intimidating that I just have to put it out here, amidst the fear, amidst the internal judgment and criticism.

I need love. I need warmth, human warmth. I need safety. I need security. I need to feel cared for. I need to feel that I matter, that I am important to somebody else. I need people around me that I can trust. I need people who I can depend on. I need to feel my own vulnerability without feeling threatened.

I am afraid of being alone. I am afraid of nobody liking me. I am afraid of people hating me or fearing me. I need to feel accepted. I need to feel appreciated. I need to feel fulfilled. I need to feel my own love. My soul needs to be free. I need to feel the liberty of movement, of confidence, of trust and love from within.

I need to be me.

There you have it. A man being honest about what his needs feel like and look like from inside his person."

You will likely feel despair. That's ok. Empty and lonely, it will seem like the world is destroying you, that life hates you. I hear you. If I could be there to give you a pat on the back or a hug I would. I know exactly how it feels. I am feeling it right now.

If you like writing, or find it cathartic or therapeutic, do it. Lots of it. Write until your mind is tired. That's why I am here. I'm writing it all out. I have decided to write each and every time that I start to feel really bad. Quite quickly I have found myself writing even when I don't feel bad. It is as if I have opened a spigot and now the water is flowing strongly. That's what we want. Flow.

Life will happen to you whether you want it to or not. The sun will rise and set with or without you every single day. This is about empowerment. Finding your strength without others, from the inside. It is most likely tied in some way to why you are reading this book in the first place. Something drove you to where you are, and it is key that you work on your responsibility within that sequence of events.

<u>Situate Yourself</u>

This book is about *you*, not the person who left you. This book is *for* you. Read it five times, read it ten times. Study it. Meditate on it. Sleep on it. Make it useful for you. I am giving you all that I have to give right now, and given that you are in a similar situation, you surely can appreciate how much of an effort that is here and now. Capitalize on my efforts.

My goal is to make you better. And make myself better at the same time. That's what we want, right? Feel better, live better. The goal here isn't to get the person back. That may happen, or it may not happen. It surely isn't the focus here. Perhaps when you finish this text you will understand why that is. You are in pain. That's what we are dealing with here.

And so am I. I am in so much pain that sometimes I have to completely stop whatever it is that I am doing in order to cope. I have advised everyone around me of what I am going through, and I think that one of the reasons for that is so that they don't freak out if/when I look like I am about to fall apart. Because I am cracking up a bit. It is part of it.

Your current situation is a direct result of a past situation. Pay attention to the fact that something vital needs to be addressed here so that it doesn't get repeated in the future. Make this work for you. Grow.

Just don't avoid the uncomfortable stuff. Distraction isn't really the answer here. It is more about survival and willingness to be where you are. For me, sometimes that means pulling over my vehicle while I am driving, and bawling my eyes out. Or not being able to spend time with friends, and telling them that I just can't. They understand or they don't.

One of the hardest things is not to chase your former partner. It is killer! A very wise man once told me that if someone doesn't want to speak to you, and you try to force them, the best outcome that you could possibly get is that they pretend to listen. That's a terrible result. More likely, if you call her or him, they will tell you that they need space and ask you nicely or not nicely to stop calling them. And now, you find yourself even further away from them, because they not only are seeking space and distance, but you just confirmed to them that they may want even more. Chasing makes them run more. Not to worry though, since you have more than enough work to do on yourself. Have patience.

Take care of yourself. Tend to yourself. You are wounded. Love hurts something awful sometimes! Rest. Have a bath. Take some naps. Take lots of walks. Long, meandering walks. Have no distance or time in mind if you can. Just wander a bit. The movement itself will be soothing. If you start obsessing about the person as you walk, don't worry too much about it. It will pass. Everything passes eventually. Your goal here is to make it through to that 'eventually' and then continue forward.

Sometimes you will be sure that you just cannot take anymore. Be willing to feel exactly that. Be willing to be overwhelmed, even if just for an instant. Sample it. Test your courage, you'll be very surprised at how much you have inside of you. Human beings have a tremendous capacity for pain. Watch what happens when you take this approach of conscious courageousness, it is really interesting and worth paying attention to. Develop an appetite for it. Be tempered in your expectations, since there is no rush.

You see, life is really funny like that. Our emotions and our thoughts react to our disposition toward them. Strange, right? What might be experienced as pain by one person could possibly be experienced with wonder and amazement by another. I noticed that this is true for many anxiety sufferers (I have struggled with anxiety for a number of years). Sometimes, what is felt as panic and anxiety for one person is the same energy and emotion that other people feel as a sort of enlightenment or spiritual high. But the trick is in the perspective and attitude. Many things are far more neutral than we realize.

Have you ever heard the idea that if you change your thoughts, that the entire world will change before your eyes? What are you thinking about these days? I'm going to guess that your thoughts are disproportionately focused on your attachment and loss of your most wonderful partner. Makes sense. Such a huge presence cannot be removed without a huge, gaping hole left behind. You are experiencing the hole. *What are you feeling*?

In my case it is a consuming, anxious, and persistent butterflies in my stomach type of sensation. I feel like everything inside me is in motion and there is a strong uncertainty as to which direction that everything is heading. I am everywhere and nowhere all at once and I am standing on jelly and everything is unstable. Pretty unpleasant place to be. Feels hellish.

Make no mistake, I am not an expert here. The truth is that I have no idea what I am doing here. I am trying to do my best to be honest and open and vulnerable, and my hope that is that by doing so, my journey will be helpful to others.

It has been really, really hard the past few days. Every couple of hours or so, I am overtaken by emotion and I just stop what I am doing and cry my eyes out for a minute or two. It is cathartic and someone told me yesterday that crying is sort of the way that we metabolize loss.

I don't know. All I know is that when it arrives I move into it suddenly and allow it to flow. I have no choice.

I often feel like Sisyphus, rolling my rock up the hill, only to have it roll back down once I am finished the task. The emotions are relentless in their endlessness.

The way through is the direct experience of wherever we are, right now. Many parts of life are painful and involve deep suffering. I have found that resisting these phases only makes things worse.

I went to a therapist the other day, and her advice was for me to feel sad for a few days. How's that for advice? But it is true, there isn't anything **TO DO** other than that in the times that the feelings are everything and they extend across the entire panorama of what I see.

With some time, maybe a good chunk of time, space will begin to appear between the waves of despair. I have already witnessed the beginning of this process. I have started to gravitate away from a place of fear and sadness. **Soooo** slowly. But what I have seen is that those feelings are loosening their grasp on my heart and my mind. What has begun to filter in is acceptance, a tiny bit of gratitude, and a smidgen of forgiveness (for her and for me).

It took me a week and a half to profoundly come to terms with the fact that my wife has indeed left me. I had found an imaginary refuge where I was hiding in the hope of returning to something that was ultimately toxic to both my wife and myself. You see, breakups don't come out of nowhere, even though they may seem to (at least to one of the parties, specifically the person who is abandoned). They usually come from behaviors between the two people that aren't healthy or conducive to the happiness and freedom of the people inside the relationship.

So even if the two people somehow find a path toward reconciliation, those elements must be purged from the relationship in order for any viable and enjoyable future to have a chance of existing.

In my case I am basically letting the reconciliation idea be free to fly away. If it comes to pass, in some future moment, then I will address it and engage it ***then and there***. My focus here and now is in achieving a relationship of peace and respect with the mother of my child to be.

I feel guilty about talking to all my friends and family non-stop about my situation and for telling them how terrible I feel. I have begun to make a concerted effort to go beyond myself and offer my own listening for their lives and stories. The people who are giving of themselves to help and support and love me are still human beings. While they are capable of exclusively listening to me, I try to only ask that of them when I absolutely need it. I love them and give them whatever little energy and love that I am able to reciprocate in the talks and encounters. Even if just a little, the effort goes a long way. I struggle with the idea of being a burden. This effort to give back helps me with that.

Give what you can. You may feel barren and weak, but love is amazingly nourishing, especially from this place. Don't be fooled by the appearances of defeat and hopelessness. Your own love is what will buoy you up to the surface from these dark depths. Get in touch with it and nurture it, revel in your own capacity to love. What you mistakenly thought was only love for that very special person, was all along your own heart beating powerfully inside your entire being, in and of itself. You are closer to being free.

Like I said earlier, I am not a therapist or counselor. I am a man, with a broken heart, navigating the waters of my breakup. If even a tiny part of this can make a difference in your experience, for the better, then I will have achieved something remarkable. Something noble.

<u>Fear</u>

I want to speak a bit here about fear. It is paralyzing. And it is very possible, even likely, that the reason that you are here, reading these words, is because you have lost the connection with your own power – you have become afraid.

Nobody is attractive when they are fearful. Our energy contracts and we imagine ourselves as tiny and helpless. Who would be drawn to that?

It starts with our own image of ourselves. Our personal narrative, if you wish to put it that way. In my case, my wife became the center of attention and the star of my show somehow. Don't get me wrong, she is beautiful and smart and intuitive and spontaneous and all sorts of sugar and spice and everything nice. I love her to bits. But she can never be the star of my narrative, or things will go sour quite quickly. Nobody but me should hold the center of my storyline. This isn't selfish; to the contrary it is honest. It reflects an appreciation of the fact that if I am unwell, then that implies that I can no longer serve my loved ones in a healthy and constructive fashion.

Our internal power, that which fuels our drive toward our goals and our achievements, is primarily our own and is not designed to be transferred to another person. Yet I did that in my relationship and I see people do it all the time in their relationships. Maybe it comes from insecurity, or a weak self-image? Maybe a person who was never taught how to profoundly value themselves is saddled with the great need for external approval?

Let me be really clear here. Until you immerse yourself in this and reclaim your strength, your power, your drive, your inspiration, discovering your immense ability to act in this world without the need for **anybody** else…until you begin to make this leap into the apparent uncertainty of your own potential, you will remain completely stuck where you are. In your life, in your relationships, in your dreams, in your achievements.

I found myself full of fear and doubt last night. I broke one of the rules and I sent a Whatsapp text message to my wife. I had spoken with a friend that we have in common (a woman) who had suggested that a short, playful message would probably be helpful in establishing contact. Maybe I just wanted to believe that so that I could break the rule and chase after my wife a bit, seeking contact.

So I sent a short message, something along the lines that I was heading to our favorite restaurant, that maybe she should meet me there (a joke since she is about a hundred miles away at her mother's home), that we could share a soup, and that I missed her. She saw the message and replied about four hours later. She told me that she missed me too, but that it didn't change the fact that we wouldn't be sharing soups anymore, and that I should not make this process harder than it need be.

And there it was. The wind from my sails gone and my boat isolated and alone in the water. And it was my fault.

I chatted with a few people about what happened to see what their opinions would look like. The harshest commentary came from a close friend who always tells me things directly, without sugarcoating it. He said that instead of inspiring and eliciting love, I was bringing up pity inside her, that she pitied me. That I was pushing her further away, coming from a place of weakness, pleading and begging. He said that I need to stop chasing and to let go, to give her the gift of missing me. It hit home, deeply. I felt dejected, powerless, pissed off at myself for not having had the ability to stick to my guns.

And here's the crux of it: It comes from not realizing my own power. Not knowing, inside of myself, what I am worth and how great that is. This is not to be confused with arrogance, it is more like a tremendous confidence that is peppered with humility so that it is noble. It is my manhood, my essence. And I had given it away, to someone else, in this case my wife. I had castrated myself basically.

It is so easy to let fear win, to give in to intimidating life tasks or situations. It is infinitely easier to run away than it is to stick around and be present for whatever is right in front of your face. It takes courage, of course it does. But without this particular courage, the person leaving you will only be one in a long list of things that you should concern yourself with. Your present situation is your golden opportunity. Take advantage of what you can achieve here.

The cool part of this is that you don't need permission from anybody to take this power and run with it. *You don't need anybody else to feel good. You never have.* Let me say that again so that it can begin to sink in. *Nobody in this world, not one soul, nobody but yourself has control over how you feel.* Weakness stems from the idea that other people can wield our power and have some sort of authority or control over it. It is an illusion. It is a lie that we tell ourselves to justify why we aren't living the life that we want. With the person that we want to live it with. And in the way that we want to live it.

Let me go deeper. The absence of personal power is what makes the gaping hole in your heart so damn painful. Don't get me wrong, there would still be plenty of pain and sadness, even with tremendous self-worth and self-love. But the experience would be distinct, very distinct. In my case I put my wife at the center of my storyline. I neglected my professional career and dreams, not because of her, but because of me. I wasn't properly taking care of my mind or body, not because of her, but because of me. I wasn't feeling full of potential and energy. I fell into routine and instead of making my own dreams and goals a reality; I spent the majority of my time supporting hers. There is nothing wrong with being a supportive spouse, and by all means definitely be there rooting for them and helping them along – but not in place of your own path. We each have our own calling, and that is a strong part of what makes us tick day to day, it is how people experience us, how people see us, respect us, are drawn toward us. Lose that and you begin to lose yourself.

Take this time to really re-direct all your focus back on to yourself. I don't recommend making any major decision in the early goings, in the first few weeks at least – those weeks should be reserved for the 'mourning' of your loss. But dip your toes in it a bit. How do you feel about your life? Specifically, and importantly, the parts that have to do with your path and not your partner. What about your body? Your habits? Your inspiration? Do you have dreams? Goals? Aspirations? Unfulfilled paths that you have always wanted to explore?

Life has body-checked you here, slammed into your story, and where you thought that you were going is gone. Read that again. *You are no longer headed where you thought that you were heading*. Perhaps you never were headed that way, more on that later. So now what?

I have found myself desperate for guidance. I listen attentively to family and friends, focus on the words of my therapist, try my very best to get some sense of where to go, and how to go there. This is a place of groundlessness, like standing on quicksand. Time to learn how to float, how to fly even. Don't limit yourself here, in fact it is important to realize that that is part of how you got here in the first place.

I was talking about fear. My wife wrote me an eight page letter detailing just about everything that she was fed up with regarding me personally and our relationship in general. There was clearly a recurrent theme of my fearfulness in the face of life and my own challenges. It had a lot of resonance for me. Some of the letter is just her own stuff, but there are also helpful elements for me in there. After all, she is the single best source of outside data on my actions and behaviors and patterns in the world. She is the only person who has been next to me, quite consistently, first as my girlfriend and then my wife, for over three years now.

Sometimes life places you on a precipice. Your heart beats faster, your mind starts racing, fear begins to grab hold everywhere. Suddenly, in flows courage, awareness, trust, worthiness, power. And the only thing that you need to do is propel yourself forward, face the fear head-on, and enjoy the ride. You jump. So I did.

This morning I did something that has terrified me for years, something that I have only held as an idea that I would love to be able to, one day, experience. I had always told those close to me that I would go and do it all alone one day and then tell them about it afterward. And that is precisely what I did. I drove down the coast, parked my car, got all geared up with the protective safety gear, and I bungee jumped over the ocean!

Wow. Wow. Wow. Wow!

I have never been so afraid. I struggled to even be able to walk into the bungee jump place. I was terrified, horrified, completely saturated with my own fear. And I jumped. I jumped! I have never, in such a quick flash, felt so much of my lost inner power be suddenly returned to me. I reclaimed my life force.

You don't have to go to such an extreme to get this, but I would certainly recommend that you challenge yourself. Do something on your own, without help. Learn something, cook something, take a trip that you always wanted to take, face a fear that you always wanted to face. Give yourself a reward just for the sole purpose of enabling yourself to receive something wonderful from your own self. Provide yourself with a show of love from within. I cannot emphasize enough how empowering this is.

The Next Day

Here I am, one day later, feeling heartbroken again. Yup. This morning I am full of resentment and bitterness and emptiness. Maybe an equal dose of each. I cannot believe that my wife lied so much to me in our relationship. So many lies, so much information also that she never even told me. Deception via false information and the withholding of relevant information. I am trying my best not to take it personally. Not easy. It is so much easier to point my finger and project the blame outward.

It would be easy for me to say that you shouldn't do this. It would be easy to say that I shouldn't either. It is also true. But here I am doing it. Have room for spite and hate and resentment and bitterness and a whole host of unpleasant feelings. Feel them all as freely as you feel sadness and despair. There is room for all of these characters within the drama of your story.

Sounds like a perfect time to talk about forgiveness and acceptance, especially toward one's self. I don't expect to be perfect, nor do I expect to do this process perfectly (*whatever that means*). I don't expect you to be perfect either. We are all flawed. We are all broken to a certain extent. Life is tricky, and we all make mistakes on a fairly constant basis. There must be room in our lives for falling down, getting things wrong, failures, and mistakes. Otherwise we get caught up in the perfectionist's loop of constant disappointment in some area of our lives. In my life, I very often found myself feeling 'not good enough' because I could always find aspects of my life that weren't the way that I wanted them to be. And in focusing my attention on those shortcomings, I would divert my attention from appreciating the various elements that were excellent and wonderful. It is like a mental trick to always stall the inflow of happiness, and to have our attention directed toward disappointment.

This is something that I need to work on, and surely anybody reading this book could benefit from a dose of self-acceptance and self-forgiveness. It is hard to resist the temptation of seeking blame in this moment. Almost in a desperate search to identify the source of the pain, as if trying to blame myself or her, as if it would change the present situation and somehow magically make it feel better. Like I said earlier in this book, accountability is healthy, but shame and guilt are not particularly helpful.

This is the breakup book. Your companion through the heartache. Your pillow to rest your head on after you have tired from crying so much. There may be times when this is your friend or your confidant or your guide. Ideally this can work wonders for your well-being. That is my hope at least. As close as I can possibly become, via my words, to being your friend and support, well that's as far as I am trying to go with this. Let these pages absorb your tears. Let the book hug your heart with its words, with its very existence. If even a drop of love can be squeezed out of this thing, that will provide you with even a tiny bit of solace, of respite from the suffering, then that is my greatest wish. I am here with you, on this path, braving the icy winds of being left alone to fend for yourself. Except that in some way I am accompanying you through this passage.

Life has plans for you. I assure you of this. Your despair will soften. Your anger and resentment will ease. Your tension, your fear, your preoccupation, all these things will begin to fade. There **will** come a day, not too far away, when light will creep back into the crevices of your heart. You will love again. I know that these words may seem like distant echoes in a barren valley, but part of you knows them to be true. The part of yourself that lies deep in your core, the part that watches and stays quiet, the part that holds your most relevant wisdom – that part is where this answer lies. We want to visit that part together, and make a ritual of it, to have it be full of reverence and humility. That part of ourselves can only be accessed by silence and listening. In this instant I would imagine that your mind is racing something awful. It will take quite a bit of work, and feeling lots of stuff on the inside, to get there.

You see, we need to get to work on all the clutter inside of you. The thoughts and the feelings. Both are very important and both are clogging up your ability to be yourself in this world. In fact, by engaging a lot of this, mostly the feelings, you will **become** yourself in the world. This is a sort of birth, or re-birth. From the ashes of your old self will rise something greater, something more pure, more refined, more beautiful. You may not see it just yet, but watch for its appearance on your horizon, because once you catch a glimpse of this person, you will smile and look forward to your future once again. Hope and inspiration will return to your center. You will move once again *with* life, instead of resisting it like you are surely doing right here and now.

Holding on, when life has moved on, causes pain. It is like being in some white water rapids, with the current rushing in one direction with tremendous force and momentum, and you are hanging on to the root of a tree, in a desperate attempt to change the inevitability of your uncomfortable, forced movement downstream. You need to learn to let go, to go with the current, even if it feels really terrible. Because this is a scenario that has moved beyond your control, beyond your wishes and desires for it to be something else. And instead of seeing what is before your eyes, you insist on thinking about what was and what could have been.

I am exactly here also. It is so hard for me to come to terms with the truth. I have been mentally rejecting the fact that she is gone, that she no longer wants to be in this marriage. It hurts so much! But no matter how bad it feels, no matter how much I rationalize and dissect the facts, analyze them to exhaustion, no matter what I do, I can't bring her back. I don't control her or her thoughts or her feelings. There is so much power in this. Yet I struggle so much doing the exact opposite of surrendering here to my circumstance. I am fighting reality, and that never ever ends well.

There is a mourning period for the loss of the love and the relationship. It is mostly a matter of time. If you insist on having expectations as to when it will end for you, please trust me when I suggest that you over-exaggerate to the lengthy side. Otherwise it will just be more frustrating, more exhausting, and more painful. It isn't really up to us the speed and intensity with which we heal from such a great heartache.

<u>Doing the Work</u>

While it isn't always possible to do anything about our external situation, we can always do work on our interior world. Specifically, it is always possible to make slight shifts in our perspective and attitude. And while they may seem like baby steps, baby steps may be exactly what the doctor ordered for you in this fragile state.

I did some intense therapy work a few days ago. It involved cathartic expressions of anger and sadness, centered within some grounding physical body work. It is called Core Energetics and I highly recommend it. I realized that I had a vast accumulation of built up anger. That may seem obvious to people looking at me from the outside these days, but it wasn't obvious for me at all. The release was wonderful, and while I didn't change anything about my outside circumstance (my wife has still left me, she's coming to get the rest of her stuff out of the house in the next few days, my heart is shattered), it dramatically moved where I am inside of me. The effect was profound.

Almost as if by magic, my struggling business got two calls for jobs in the past two days. I swear it was as if the very moment that I decided to care about **me,** to take care of **me,** the universe reacted immediately. My sister says that I became magnetic in the moment that I invested into myself. Reading this book is a clear investment into your own well-being. Be happy about that. Let me tell you why you should be happy that you are showing up for yourself here.

We wake up alone. Until we open our eyes and simultaneously allow the flood of sensory stimuli to flow inward, we have a moment of just being, within ourselves. It is private and personal and takes place 100% within our own being. When we sleep it is the exact same thing. Also when we die. The very nature of our primary existence before we interact with our world and our surroundings is aloneness. Solitude. Many people distract themselves with external things with the goal of avoiding the sort of emptiness within, the essential void within us that reminds of the impermanence of our world and ourselves. But it won't go away, and there is something truly remarkable to be experienced if you stop hiding from it.

Make friends with yourself. You are where everything starts and ends. Take care of that core essence that resides deep within you. If you value yourself and work on yourself, the world will change before your eyes. I know, I know, it sounds like cheesy new age fluff. Try it out. Close your eyes. Just watch and feel what's going on when you begin to look inward. You'll find that most, if not all, of the issues that you have with the world source themselves in what you are experiencing just sitting or lying down on your own, inside yourself. It may take a great deal of watching and listening in this sacred place for you to get better clarity, but it is always a good time to start. Learn to meditate. Learn to be quiet. Learn to pay attention to what **really** makes you happy and what **really** makes you sad. Teach yourself to listen to your own inner voice.

You are not here by chance. For whatever reason, your life and how you live it brought you exactly to this moment along your path. Make the pain and hurt useful, since it is going to immerse you in it either way. You might as well gain something here.

Listen, nobody is going to do any of this for you. I cannot emphasize this enough. It is entirely up to **you** how far and how high you will fly in your life. It is up to you how you bounce back from this and what it all means to you. Don't let this experience close your heart. Don't let this experience diminish your dreams, your goals, or your aspirations. Don't allow your context to make you feel small and inadequate. I would suggest that you consider the possibility that all of these things that I am recommending for you to avoid already have a foothold in your life and are likely connected to how you got here in the first place. And it is not because you suck, because you don't. But you are doing a few things wrong. And today is when you begin to change. How exciting, right? Imagine that, a glimmer of excitement in the middle of this dark space. Believe it!

Take this opportunity to think about what you want in this life. Who do you want to be? How do you want to be? How do you want to feel? Make a few lists. Truly evaluate all aspects of your life. Don't go changing everything around just yet though. Making huge life decisions in a place of trauma is ill advised. But you can gear up for them, orientate your life toward where you would like to be. Make the big decisions in a few weeks, or maybe even in a few months from now. If it makes you feel better, you can strongly contemplate the ideas, just refrain from jumping just yet. Maybe just feel the potential of these new possibilities, the warm optimism that surrounds being a better version of yourself. I think of this like revving your own engine. You get to feel how powerful you are, how much control you have over changing your world. It returns you to your power source, your strength. Because that is something that many people fail to realize in these tough times.

This is about whatever you want it to be about. You are free. It may not feel great, not just yet. But it will. You will leave this experience with so much more than you entered it with. You have no idea how important this juncture is in your life. You are just beginning to contextualize it. Can you feel it? That gentle purr of your engine. Be in that, feel that. Get close to it, it is your center. Nobody can take that from you. Nobody ever could, it is just that perhaps you abandoned it and forgot that it was yours. And that's fine. We all screw up, often in fact.

I want you to feel awesome about who you are by the time that you finish this book. I know, what a huge stretch, right? No way, you say. I feel terrible, you say. My heart is empty. My partner crushed me, abandoned me, left me to rot and die. I hear you. But the bad stuff, the really horrible stuff that you are going through, it will have an end. It will release you. And I want you to be ready to hit the ground running whenever that happens. I want you to start getting your traction now. Empower yourself with all of these ideas. Another thing, you'll find that as you go further into healing yourself and learning your strength, you will become much more attractive to others. People want to be around others that make them feel good. It is a very basic law of human interaction. If you feel better inside of you, those around you will feel better being near you. Also, the same principle applies to the contrary, being that if you are all closed up and feeling tiny, people will pity you and maybe feel bad for you, but they surely won't feel empowered by hanging around you. Change yourself and everybody shifts with you. Your world changes too, for the better.

Do you see it yet? Do you see what I have been alluding to this entire book? Have you heard your head click into the idea? It has always been under your control. Your happiness, your general health, your success, your confidence, your magnetism. Nobody can take it away or build it up, except you. Nobody can make you shine except you. If someone dear to you says something wonderful to you, and you feel great upon hearing it, you are deciding to shine. You are taking their commentary as the perfect excuse to feel great. See it for what it is, which is *your choice to make you feel good*. Once you really key into this, your life will never go back to where it was before this.

Life is giving you a shot here, a real shot, to change something essential about yourself that has caused you to be in relationships that didn't work and have life patterns that didn't serve you. Yes, this is **this** big of a deal here. Run with it. And never look back. And once this book no longer serves you, give it to someone else that needs it. Pass it along and enable another person's escape from their own hole that they have dug over years or decades.

Life is short. So short. We don't realize it often until something goes horribly wrong, often the tragic loss of a loved one. I bore witness firsthand to this when my wife lost her father to a heart attack. It was horrendous, so much pain, so much crying. I stood by her side and just tried to be her rock, hugging her when she needed it, being strong when she needed me to be. Just being available basically for her for an extended period. One thing that I learned is that we have no idea whatsoever how long we have left here. This truth serves well as the impetus for growing into the human being that I would prefer to be. Give yourself the biggest break of your life. You'll be scratching your head as to why you waited so long to do this. Hopefully by then you'll have no problem forgiving yourself for having taken so long. Start your life from today, from this instant. We are given what seems to be an almost endless supply of 'right now' moments, within which we can shift and turn our essential beliefs and attitudes to better suit our lives.

I was thinking today about the roles that men and women play in relationships. I think that when things are flowing nicely, the woman tends to look at her man and envision the great man that she can see him becoming. With this wonderful thought and image in her mind, she happily takes her place beside him, full of her own strength and appreciating his as well. The man, when he is in his own power and potential, radiates his goals and his life mission, his intentions are clear and strong and he is magnetic. He stands next to his woman and is a source of safety and dependability for her. These may be generalizations, but there is something very relevant to how it works.

Attraction should be earned, constantly. It should not be taken for granted. Never assume that your partner will just wake up and want to be next to you each and every day without any effort on your part. That's silly and naive. Just as you can develop attractive qualities, you can just as easily foster unattractive qualities and drive your partner away. Now that your partner has left, you are in an excellent position to work on yourself and grow your quality of person. This will have two results. First and foremost, you'll start to feel quite a bit better about yourself. You will walk with your chin up and with your outlook more constructive and forward-thinking. Next, it will make you draw people toward you.

I have lost a tremendous amount of weight in the past few weeks. The broken heart diet of never really being hungry has helped me shed the extra pounds that I had put on in recent years. It is such a strange sensation, that of feeling almost no desire to eat, an almost complete lack of appetite. And when I eat, I eat little. I had a multivitamin the other day, just to make sure that I was getting enough vitamins and minerals.

I also haven't slept well. Too many thoughts. Lots of tossing and turning, rolling about in the bed that used to be occupied by two of us, well two and a half of us to be precise. Peace of mind has abandoned me as well in these tough times.

Each day I wake up and take my dog out to the park nearby. I have made it a morning ritual to give thanks for what I have. It often is difficult and I even apologize in my mind as I think about gratitude, for not being fully able to embody gratitude while I feel so sad and depressed. It often goes something like this, "Thank you for the tremendous beauty that surrounds me, for the friends and family who have come out and shown me love and support, for the wisdom and strength that I have needed to traverse this passage. I know that I can only feel a bit of this beauty that surrounds me, that I am really limited because I just feel so bad, and I am sorry for not being able to feel more of this, but I am touching this gratitude with everything that I have available in this moment."

Maybe I could afford to lose the apology, the guilt that surrounds not feeling good enough here. Surely it doesn't serve me well. It is just that sometimes it is hard to look around where I live, a place on this earth that combines lush jungle with beautiful ocean, and find myself feeling so blue in this context. It is a sort of surreal experience similar to when you have rain but you can see the sun shining overhead.

It is challenging in my life to avoid operating from a place of fear. Fear of abandonment, fear of rejection, fear of never getting my wife back, fear of being so distant from my soon to be born baby. There is a long list of things to be fearful of, should I desire to pay attention to them. Sometimes it gets a stranglehold on me and I just have to give up and let go. I breathe deeply and then give myself a new opportunity to engage my reality a few moments later.

Not all thoughts can be easily brushed aside. Some of the scarier ones tend to grab hold for longer periods, starting a spiral into more complex and intimidating ideas. These thoughts feed on our attention and our energy. Don't expect to beat them all. Actually, in the first part of this process, you may find yourself almost a slave to many of them. That's ok. It feels treacherous, but it's fine. You'll need to recalibrate what's 'fine' in your world right now to cover quite a bit more territory. It is just part of it.

There isn't a correct way to do this, it isn't some type of exact formula that you can follow and everything turns out just peachy. Life just doesn't work that way, not from what I have seen at least. I have already made tons of 'mistakes' with my wife since her departure. I have done things that friends and therapists have told me not to do under any circumstance, and I also have done things that I even state here should be avoided. And that's important to note. The idea is to make sure that your general direction is correct, that the sum of all your actions are at least heading in the direction that you seek. And to be honest, even if you royally screw this up and do everything catastrophically wrong, well…you'll get another chance in your next relationship to do things differently.

Just be kind to yourself. Forgive the mistakes as they happen, if you can. Give yourself *a **huge amount of leeway***. Allow room for giant mistakes and be ready for a few do-overs as you fumble around with this. This is life, nobody gets it perfectly right. But you love her/him you say! This is the one! You couldn't possibly imagine being without them! I get it. That doesn't mean that it won't happen. Those words sting, don't they? Maybe you even are developing a touch of resentment toward me for having said it.

Try to approach the idea slowly at first if you want. Consider, for a moment, that this is truly the very end of your relationship. That he or she is never coming back. Try to touch it as often as you can, allow the tears, allow the pain. Cry. A lot. Letting go is not easy and you are not expected to be a martyr with the hardship that this brings with it. The process will take as long as it needs to for you.

Whether or not your partner returns and there is some sort of reconciliation is actually tied to your capability to let them go completely. It may seem counterintuitive, but it is true. In all likelihood, your emotional hooks into them are unhealthy at this point. For whatever reason, they left you, and it is a safe bet that it isn't because you were not holding on to them tight enough. The higher probability is that you were holding on to them too tightly. People tend to get caught up in push and pull relationships and what one partner does, the other does the opposite. At least when we are looking at excesses. So if one partner won't let go and is always chasing, the other will probably flee and push away, and vice versa.

Find what you are doing too much of, and take it down many notches. Stop if you can. Take your time. Be patient. Breathe. This may be slow goings.

The Gambler

Before I go any further, I want to introduce a strange concept – that of breaking the rules. Don't do this until you are really in good contact with your feelings and your heart. Wait until you have a good sense of clarity, or this will be harmful for your desired outcome.

Sometimes our gut tells us something distinct to what would appear to be the best course of action. Be **VERY** careful here. It is imperative that you are able to distinguish between your pain and suffering and what are signals from your intuition. Your gut is to be trusted, <ins>as long as you can listen to it properly</ins>. If you have doubts, then maybe a little waiting is in order. It is *generally* best to err on the side of caution.

But it may come to pass that you need to do something that makes no sense to you or that you just feel is what you need to do. That's your sign. There is a subtle sensation of certainty within powerful gut impulses. And while I say that you should err on the side of caution, I also realize that we only live once and that courage is usually rewarded. My advice, however tricky a situation that it may put you into, is to go ahead and do it. I believe that our connections with other people are complex and operate on levels that we don't see and sometimes cannot perceive. When two people nurture and develop a connection over time, the bond kind of becomes its own entity. The love between you, so to speak, begins to have a life of its own. And both of you can tap into it and listen to it, since therein lies abundant wisdom about what both of you want and need from yourselves and each other. Trust and have some faith in your ability to develop insights into this elusive source of information.

You need to learn to listen here. Listen to what your partner is telling you, either by their actions alone or by their words and actions. Listen to what you are telling yourself, deep down. Close your eyes and spend plenty of time in silence, in your solitude, just paying attention and listening to the murmurs of your own internal dialogue. Stop the otherwise noisy chatter in your head, or at least allow it to be soothed and calmed. It just clutters up your ability to hear what is being spoken to you from the part of you that holds your greatest wisdom.

You currently find yourself at a juncture in your life. You stand before a fork in the road. How you walk forward here will mark something significant in your development as a healthy and confident human being. Take it seriously, you owe it to yourself to try hard here and put in a good effort. How many times in your life have you had a golden opportunity to shift some things and live distinctly to how you were living before? How many times have you had doors of opportunity that were open before you and you ultimately chose not to enter the place of the unknown that lies beyond them? How many times have you jumped from the cliffside, toward the void, without any guarantee of success?

It may seem like the least likely spot in your life to find courage. I know. But you would be very surprised to realize what you are actually capable of here and now. First choose to act, then wonder about whether or not you feel 'up to it.' I am not kidding. Our minds tend to trail our ability to act. They watch and then react to what we do. If you have ever done something very daring or scary you have seen this effect. You go and do the thing, and it is almost as if you are in this intense surreal dream state, with your mind observing from a distance. Adrenaline pumping, you can revel in the experience, and once it is complete, *only then* will your mind rush in to analyze everything. After the fact.

I want to speak a bit now about the difference between **what I want** and **what is**. There is always a gap, more like a valley, between what is directly in front of my eyes and that which I would prefer to see and experience. The extent of this difference is often the direct source of my suffering. Let me give a few examples.

I find myself alone without my wife. I really want my wife to be here with me, touching me, holding me, loving me. By not letting go of the desire, or the wanting of something that I do not have, I feel the pain of its absence. If I refuse to operate from a place of truth, of honesty with respect to **what is**, I will suffer.

Another example: I make plans with a friend to go to a movie at 4pm. On the way to the theater, I get caught in traffic and end up having to rush. My stress levels go up and I become more focused on getting there on time. I drive too close to the curb, my tire bangs it hard and my tire blows out. I begin to get irate and have a bad reaction. The gap between arriving at the movie on time and enjoying myself (*what I want*)…and where I find myself changing a tire and missing the entire experience (*what is*), is very large.

One last example: Let's say that I refuse to let go of the last truly happy experience that I shared with my wife. Instead of being in the place that I am now, which is on my own and without my wife, I mentally insist on holding on dearly to this past event as if it were feasible to bring it into the present moment and to go so far as to **replace** my undesirable present moment with this memory. This is a recipe for pain.

I need to begin from a place of sincerity. How do I feel? What is my present circumstance? What does my heart feel here and now? If I am unwilling to start from these questions, I have a fairly high likelihood of avoiding my truth and instead latching on to fantasies. And that's the last thing that I want here because it will inevitably equate to more pain, more suffering. While suffering and pain is part of this, surely I don't want to generate more than the necessary amount, right? I think so.

So, if I am not believing my situation, am in denial or am mentally rejecting it to the point that I instead choose to hook into a bunch of things that either already happened or may never happen, I begin to travel far away from anything tied to *what is* within my life landscape. I do this all the time. I won't lie. I don't like my options, so I imagine other ones or refuge myself in fake ones. Bad recipe. Guaranteed outcome that sucks.

Another thing that I find myself doing a lot of these days is trying to rationalize my way through this entire thing. The misguided intention that I harbor in those moments is to think my way through it, especially the sticky and uncomfortable emotions. Attempting to process **feelings** with **thoughts** is a good way to get filled with anxiety and nerves. Feelings are meant to be felt, that is precisely how we process them. Try running your car on salt or sugar instead of gasoline and you will get a great lesson in why certain processes require specific inputs with specific destinations.

If possible, find out from your partner who has left exactly why it is, in their mind and heart, that they left. Be generous when asking for this information, and try to avoid resentment and conflict. The goal is to gather some relevant data as to where **they** think that something went wrong. Your partner may blame you, or blame themselves, or have a multitude of beliefs as to why the relationship fractured. It is helpful to try and hear the other person's point of view. Be cautious though, since the information will come with a bias and a clear perspective that is not yours. It also may be jaded and could be highly charged with emotions that trigger things for you. I expect that any reply will be very difficult for you to hear. Be calm and do your best to receive the words. The point is **not** whether or not they are right. Learn to steer clear of those sort of qualifiers, as well as the desire to determine who is right and who is wrong.

You should find out what their experience was and see what it looks like. You have your own story, your own narrative of how things unfolded. Surely it contrasts with what they believe and are telling themselves. Learning the differences, and attempting to extend beyond yourself and into their vantage point is a healthy exercise. You need this skill in order to be able to better communicate.

I have been on a quest to accumulate information and wisdom here. Clearly I am in a spot where everything appears to have halted, and now requires maintenance, in my world. I like to consider this point as being akin to a person who is scaling a mountain. They get tired, they lose their wind for a moment, and they stop to take a breath. This is my breath. Recovery, recuperation, rest, regroup, relaxation, and off I go once again.

The overwhelming pangs of pain and sadness have become less intense.

Control, Trust & Respect

"There is a crack, a crack in everything, that's how the light gets in." -Leonard Cohen

I want to talk about control and respect in relation to my spouse and in relation to my life. This is a fairly extensive subject and I hope that I am able to properly do it justice.

When I operate from fear, I attempt to control the people and events in my environment. It is an exhausting effort that leaves everybody who is involved annoyed and asphyxiated by my actions. I have historically been overbearing and meddling with both my wife and my son, both to great measures. There are a few things that lie directly behind this attempt to control that which cannot be controlled.

I grew up in a difficult atmosphere. My parents tended towards fighting with one another and also had little if any time for us, their children, on a day to day basis. Both of my parents worked very hard and were out of the house most of the day, as such I was mostly brought up by babysitters. Interestingly enough, on a side note, many of these women (they were all women) came from Caribbean countries. And since they had mostly free reign over the food that they would prepare for us kids, I grew up eating lots of mango and plantain and curry stews. Yummy. But my parents were never there for the meals. Maybe we had one or two meals together a week as a family that I can remember. In short, I grew up with a fragmented and not dependable family unit that was also often abrasive and threatening to me. I woke up very often late at night to the scary sounds of my mother and father having very heated arguments and disagreements. I experienced a lot of anxiety and fear as a child. The context didn't exactly nurture my becoming an adult man that trusts his world. To the contrary. Only now, as a grown man, am I beginning to learn to grow and trust within my world and to finally discard all those habits of self-preservation and protection that I learned as a small child in order to shield myself from my surroundings that I perceived as unstable and unsafe.

So the first crucial element is trust. If I don't trust my wife, for example, then it will cost me greatly to let go and have her live her life in our shared space freely. I will tend toward, if I am coming from this place of fear and uncertainty, being invasive and all over her about how to do each individual thing. It's unpleasant for her to experience, and horrible for me to participate in the role of watcher and supervisor. Yet there I was, doing that, many times during our marriage. Oof, what a pain in the ass I was.

The other element, and this is also a really big one, is the reality that I cannot expect my wife to act as a subservient creature, at my beckon call. In fact, each and every time that I treat her as less than the great woman that she is, I create resentment inside her. It goes beyond that. Each time that I address my wife in this way, as a person who is supposedly below me, less than me, someone who needs to serve my wishes or needs, I fail to respect and honor her power and presence in my life and in her life. This is so important and relevant to her well-being. And it plays directly into my anger and sadness tied to having been left.

You see, my wife left because she was sick and tired of behaviors that made her feel weak and small. Mine and hers. I pushed toward a scenario where she would be compromised and be forced to fit into an excruciatingly small paradigm inside my head of *how things should be*. And, of course, I would be upset every time that she wouldn't do what I wanted her to do. A very wise man who I have spoken to a lot recently told me that human beings are *chronically disobedient*. He said that I should not expect my wife to do anything even close to what I ask. That I need(ed) to learn to expect my wife to act as she sees fit. Wow, what a contrast, right?

Let's bring this back to where we are. Upset that we have been left. But think about this for a second, follow me into this. **We don't control what they do**. We can't. The moment that you find yourself trying to control your partner, you are very screwed. Not only will they disobey, because no partner should ever act as some sort of employee to their significant other, but they will hate you. Mark my words. This sort of unhealthy interaction breeds hate.

Perhaps you are angry because your partner didn't do what you want. Of course they didn't. If they were doing what you wanted, they would have stayed (without regard for how **they** felt or what **they** needed).

Ask yourself these questions, and have the courage and sincerity to hear the answers. Who wants to be left and abandoned? Are you truly trying to see where they are coming from? Why did they leave? Had they attempted to warn you prior? Were there signs? Were you even listening? Why are you surprised? They likely are **not** surprised.

What they did made sense to them, but probably made no sense to you, and caught you entirely by surprise. Imagine, for a moment here, the enormous gap in between your and your partner's perception of the events that led to you acquiring and reading this book. Take a second to consider that your frame of mind and perspective is not the only one. Your point of view may be skewed and distorted. It probably is. You may only now be coming closer to a mental and emotional place wherein you are willing to admit this to yourself. What will follow will be many tears if that is the case, and wonder, as to how you arrived where you are from a place that you **considered** to be healthy before.

In my mind, my wife wasn't as big as me. She didn't hold nearly as much space in there (in my head and in my consideration for her) and clearly I had her as less important. My actions reflected this choice. I was intimidated by her. I was afraid of her will, her strength, and her determination. I loved her passion and power, yet that was precisely what made me hold on so tight to her and limit her freedom. Interesting that the same things that drew me to her would be that which would scare me about her. But it was. So I held her and tried to influence her movements and decisions. I wanted her to fit my world, to be the woman that I needed, when I needed it. Of course I didn't have a real clue as to what that even was. But I convinced myself that exercising control was the safest and most efficient way to achieve some notion of happiness. How foolish in retrospect. How unfair and disrespectful on my part.

Of course she ran away. I would have too in her position. Who wants to be asked to be a mere shadow of themselves? Who wants to be limited and squeezed into a little box and asked to stay there and be content? God, how naïve I was. Now, in retrospect, the clarity has begun to cut away the delusions and present me with a more honest and fair assessment of the facts. And they don't play well for my story. In fact, I have had to completely rewrite the story and be willing to hold myself entirely accountable for my mistakes. Without that accountability, I limit my ability to change things.

I have begun to observe and question the idea that this situation is unfair, or that it should be different, or that she needed to act another way. These things are projections from within me, toward a woman that I have no control over, and who acts of her own accord and decides to live her life as she sees fit. She makes sense to herself. It is up to me, if I really want to listen and understand her, to figure out what that is. If I care for her, then it is my obligation to figure this out and hear what she is saying. I am here because I have failed in this respect. This explains why I am still in the dark to a certain degree about a whole host of issues. It is my one-sided internal narrative which eclipses my understanding of the entirety of my situation.

The letter that I received helped tremendously and the fact that my wife is a writer by trade helped in the eloquence and colorfulness of her descriptions and explanations. She gave me many answers. She even went into detail, and it took my looking just slightly past the harsh and enraged words to find some clues. I needed to seek out the meaning and feelings **behind** the words, the nuances and subtleties of how and why she said what she said. How sad, though, that it took us getting to this stage to be able to hear each another…and not even hear one another, this is just *me hearing her*. My lack of proper communication toward her is a totally different story.

Understand this: you and I are here, in these words and this experience because some things have gone horribly astray from where they ought to be. Unhealthy habits and communication patterns have taken over and profound changes and adjustments are required regardless of whether or not some sort of reconciliation (if that's what you want here) is to take place. Before any movement is to occur, the first and foremost act must be one of admitting to one's self what this really looks like. As opposed to how we may want it to look.

It is easy to play the part of the victim. The 'poor me' and my poor unhappy circumstance. There is place for sadness, no doubt about that. But being a victim will not empower your much needed change. It can't.

First things first, is to stop messing things up, as quickly as you can. Identify and address anything and everything that you are doing that is continuing the problems that drove your partner away. Become a professional student of your errors, of your bad habits, of your selfish and offensive tendencies. Be careful though, don't fall into fits of self-criticism and self-hate, because that's just going to set you back even further. Straight honesty coupled with a big dose of generosity and forgiveness is the name of the game here. Err on the side of being too nice to yourself here. I know that this is hard as hell. How are you supposed to assess all these screw ups without feeling like an idiot? I get it. I totally get it.

Listen. We all make mistakes. Like the Leonard Cohen quote says at the start of this section, everything has cracks, and that's where the light gets in. We are all flawed and prone to make tons of mistakes. And once we fall down, life very often provides the opportunity to learn both why we fell as well as how to avoid falling again. It requires sincerity and humility, but the lesson and its wisdom is usually there and accessible.

Figure out how to appreciate your partner again. Figure out how to honor her or his greatness. Wonder in their difference and variety. Learn to coexist with elements of this world that do not operate in the way that you do. Welcome the fact that this contrast is what is teaching you what you need to learn in order to grow. Thank them for not wanting to be like you. Thank them for showing you your limitations and shortcomings. Because they are our greatest teachers. If we are willing. If we are courageous enough to admit fault, and to strive toward something greater than ourselves, then we will work toward being a better version of ourselves.

It is time to exchange our limited and controlled past, one which was firmly locked into a debilitating and suffocating comfort zone, for an uncertain future where we get to be so much more. Free yourself here and now. These chances come around in very special passages of our lives. Seize this one and never look back. You can most definitely do this! Think of how far you have come just since you began to read this book. Congratulate yourself, and be proud of yourself. You are many steps closer to becoming the new you.

This **is** exciting. Feel it. Immerse yourself in it. You are becoming something wonderful. You are becoming a person who doesn't repeat the steps that brought them here. This is a pivotal spot in your story, one that you will look back upon with great pride. This place is where you decipher your past and where you begin programming your path going forward in a way that honors and respects both yourself and your partner. This is the way through. It is the road less travelled. With each subsequent step forward from here on in, you'll notice the shifts and the changes occurring within you. The choices that you make will be more empowered, more informed, wiser, more considerate, and more inclusive of points of view that are not your own. Your mental panorama will expand tremendously and your ability to properly consider those around you will increase manifold. This is all great stuff!

Contact, Listening, and Learning to See Clearly

So what happens if your partner gets in touch with you? Well, to start, ask questions and try to focus more on listening to them than on talking to them. Allow them to engage you. Try to learn as much as you can from the interaction, specifically focusing on why they left and what it is about either you or the relationship that really got to them.

You'll have to evaluate for yourself where things lie and whether or not your intentions will be toward reconciliation or if you are ready to let the relationship end. I can't really help you with that, except to say that you ought to be completely honest with yourself and listen very carefully to your heart. Let it be a decision that comes very little from ego, or pride. And by that I mean that it is foolish to want to return to someone who is mistreating you, or will continue to not properly value you, or someone who perhaps doesn't even love you anymore (or worse, someone who never did). Life has provided you with a rest, a moment to catch your breath in order to be able to see things more clearly. Apply that bit of clarity to your relationship and come to your own conclusion exclusive of the fact that the person left you.

You are still empowered, and there is great value in taking your own decision here, even if it almost seems symbolic to you. A relationship takes two willing parties. You are one of those two, and both your participation and commitment are vital either way to the outcome.

I don't have to do anything that I don't want to do. And I certainly am not particularly interested in having my romantic and family situation based upon obligations in place of that which satisfies and fulfills me. Life isn't perfect, but we definitely can exercise power and choice within these things. In my particular case, I want to remain married and I want to travel the road of learning and growth toward developing a new state of affairs and communication with my wife (who is presently in another city). It's a hard path, one that requires much introspection and honesty. I am struggling and pushing forward toward my goals here. I invite you to consider your choices and to begin to invest of yourself accordingly with the purpose of moving strongly in your desired direction. Clear intentions carry great power.

In my case, my wife and I did eventually speak and connect. After approximately three weeks of not hearing her voice, it was quite an impact to hear her speak again. But it wasn't like before, since we had experienced a severe break in our relationship. Our break requires a lot of follow up work in order to be able to get to a place of healthy and clear communication. And the fact is that only once we can begin to feel like we are listening and hearing and understanding each other properly can we begin to move toward bigger steps like her returning to our home and the initiation of a new chapter in our life. We aren't there yet and where we are now is oftentimes a bit exhausting and disheartening. That being said, there are bright rays of hope and possibility.

In my relationship, I have had to go through a process of tremendous vulnerability, meaning that I have had to be willing to be brutally honest with myself and my wife. Vulnerability means opening up one's self to potential harm and hurt. In order to love, we need to be willing to experience pain. If I, for example, am not open or exposed emotionally, I can't get the rewards of the love that I seek. As much as I remain guarded and with my defenses up, is equal to my limitations of connection with the person that I love. Love happens when we expose our hearts, when our most sensitive and vulnerable spots are open and recognized within our experience. This means going to that most uncomfortable place inside us and feeling what is there. That's where the power lies, and it may still seem counterintuitive to you right now.

It isn't easy to change. Especially when we are talking about deep seated habits and behavior patterns. They take time to change, sometimes months or even years. Don't expect some sort of magic transformation wherein you are suddenly a new man or woman. It doesn't really work like that. You need to start by accurately identifying that which you are doing wrong. Then stop it. Then begin to change it and replace it with healthy and constructive behaviors. Then do those over and over again until they become your new patterns. It isn't quick and instantaneous. But it is possible and if you take steps in the proper direction, the cumulative effects toward your well-being will be remarkable. Your whole world will transform into something more inspiring and enjoyable to live – mark my words.

I was serious earlier when I spoke about paying attention to what our partner points out that they didn't like about us. Our partners tend to hold a beautiful and optimistic vision of who we *could* be. And it isn't pie in the sky, it is more akin to where we will be if we make some really sound and careful decisions with our eyes directed toward a better future. So they *do* have our best interest at heart most often when they speak about things that we could change. But our pride, my lord, our pride gets completely in the way in these moments.

Who are they, we ask, to tell us how to be? What do they know about our dreams? They don't even know what we want deep down. You probably tell yourself these things, but it is mostly bullshit. It is complete and utter nonsense that you are convincing yourself of regarding your partner. They have seen you day in and day out for an extensive period of time. They have listened to you speak about yourself and your aspirations. They see into your eyes and catch glimpses of what you most want to become. And that stuff excites them, and draws them to you. It is what made them fall in love with you in the first place. And more than anything, they have dreamed of being beside you as you achieve great things. They didn't sign up for a bad ride that leads to misery. Consider that they got off the 'bus' because it no longer appears very convincing to them that you would be the man or woman that they envisioned for you.

Usually, the vision that a partner has for you is based very much on your own vision, that which you have displayed through actions and spoken of in your most private and honest moments. **Listen to them when they talk to you about how to get there!** Even if it is a conversation after she or he has left you, you will get the same information, albeit with a bit more resentment or anger (in all likelihood). In that specific scenario, it will be framed as <u>what you failed to do</u>, and <u>who you failed to be</u>. Our partners not only share a dream with us, they often lock in to that dream in a very serious way, so serious that if you fail to stay on your path, driven toward your goals, they could walk away. Crazy, right? Once you begin to see these things from this new perspective, you will find it easier to understand how you arrived here and how you will be able to leave this place confidently.

Time for me to talk about something really subtle and sneaky. I noticed that something has been plaguing my thoughts and experiences in recent weeks. It has taken me a while to begin to identify it and even longer to be able to admit to myself that it was actually taking place. There is not only a gap in between what I want to happen (or be happening) and the reality in which I find myself. There is another gap that is equally as important. And that is the difference between what I think is happening and what is actually happening. Whoa, is this one a crazy one! And dangerous too.

It usually has come to my attention when I am full of fear and have enough awareness to be conscious of that fact. I have found that I can generally trust my gut instincts. But I have also learned that when anxious or nervous thoughts enter my mind, that they masquerade as gut instincts. In fact, there are many times when I am unable to tell the difference. This took me a lot of effort and brutal honesty to discover. So how does this play out? What does it look like? Well, in short, my own mind can play tricks on me, fueled by negative emotions like worry and being scared, and I begin to believe that things are worse than they are. I also, at times, may imagine elements of my reality that don't even exist outside my own mind. Scary stuff. As a result, I run the very real and potentially destructive risk of **acting upon misguided or false data**.

I think that just about everybody does this to a certain extent. We are all so locked into our subjective storylines that we fail to distinguish between them and the truths held by other people in our immediate environment. This is also a semi-functional, crude explanation as to why people argue and misunderstand one another constantly in this world that we live in. But what I am getting at here is what occurs when my subjective story is *wrong*, to put it bluntly.

It happened to me yesterday. I have been quite raw, and broken down, for lack of a better way to put it, for quite a few weeks now. My emotions have run close to the surface and my sensitivity to my surroundings has been especially high. My heart has been very reactive to each little stimulus and shift. It has been exhausting mostly, but in a way it has been the most truthful and authentic time of my life. I am being completely honest with how I feel and I have been available to actually feel everything that has come up for me. But yesterday a sort of ghost emotion fooled me.

I became filled with the sensation of butterflies in my stomach. I was nervous and worried about my future with my wife. I filled myself with fear - a terrible place to operate from. It is a debilitating space where I am prone to rigidity and close-mindedness. I began to believe that if I failed to hold on tightly to my wife, that she would symbolically fly away and leave me behind. Oh, what a horrible place!

If I choose to operate from that place, I become immediately clingy and needy and I am very unattractive to those around me. Who wants to be with somebody who holds on to their arm for dear life and doesn't let go? Yuck! My experience is that people tend toward rejecting those who display those characteristics. It is the polar opposite of my 'being myself', open and relaxed and confident. Instead, my self-worth and esteem is replaced by neediness and fear.

If, and it has happened a few times in recent weeks, I choose to interact with anybody from a clingy and needy place, and the worst would be with my partner, then the following tends to happen: I latch on to them as if they were a life raft in a storm and they inevitably begin to push me away. It is human nature. When people hold on to us too tightly, we often push away from them. Nobody wants to be asphyxiated or smothered by another person, it is uncomfortable and triggers the desire to escape and run away. I understand and empathize completely that in this place where you are located; there is a certain likelihood that you will be feeling *exactly* this way and perhaps with frequency in the first few weeks. That's fine, maybe while among family and friends (or when you are alone), but please understand that it *isn't* fine with your partner. In fact, it is totally destructive.

This state is the opposite of trust. And by trust I mean trust in life, trust in yourself, and trust in your partner. Trust is a very powerful thing, since it can either open or close doors for you here. You are hurt, I understand, so trust is maybe a bit of a far reach for you here. Fine. But don't throw the distrust at your partner, ***especially if they have just ran away from you and/or the relationship***.

If you feel panicky, it is going to suck. I won't lie. You must do anything and everything *except* engage your partner from that place. If it is intense enough, you may just have to survive it. It will pass. It always does.

Your partner has probably stopped believing that the person with whom they fell in love with will ever return to their life. By that I mean that they have likely become disillusioned with you, and may not think that you can change – or worse, that you lied to them the entire time about who you are. Succinctly put, they don't believe you anymore. My wife's letter was full of that, that she didn't believe me when I said this or that, that she didn't believe me when I said that I would change, that she no longer believed that *I could* change. My fault, pretty much all of it to be honest. I wouldn't believe me either if I were in her shoes. Too many failed promises perhaps. Now I have decided to change first, and then just have her realize it without me trying to sell the idea. Proof first, words second. My bed, I made it, now I am sleeping in it.

OK, so if you are in a panicky or fearful place, a few things are happening. First and foremost, it is essential to question the assumptions going on inside your head. Watch for declarative or assertive statements in your head. Pay close attention to words like *always* and *forever* and *never* in what you are thinking. These are signs of inflexible and likely conflictive and closed positions. Really, profoundly, challenge the ideas and assumptions. They are likely lies that you are used to telling yourself, so you may be out of luck for a while since you could be totally enrolled in the storyline. This is what I was just talking about, what happens when we start believing untruths. Second, there is a good chance that your mental and emotional space is one of extreme weakness. Pathetic actually. It's true. While there is nothing wrong with hanging out in this from time to time as you heal, you need to hide it a bit, especially from your partner. This state is almost exactly the same as the one where petty fights originate. I have no problem with you being here. Just be sure to acknowledge where you are and completely refrain from communicating with your partner **from** this place. It would be toxic to do so and nothing good will come of it. The good news is that it will pass.

Your partner wants to see you thrive. Even if they have just left you. Please read these lines over and over until the light bulb turns on in your head. Your partner wants you well. They may resent you for not being well. They may hate you because they believed that you would be someone else. Who knows? That's up to you to figure out and decipher and to decide what you want to do with the knowledge eventually. But listen, and pay attention here. They want to see you at your best. In fact, that is *the only way* that you will get them back (if that's what you want). Your goal here, for **yourself**, is to remember who you are and how you deviated so much from that optimized life path (that both of you envisioned) and ended up here reading these words. If this book achieves its intended outcome, then by the end of reading this text you will be chomping at the bit and excited about filling your shoes and being completely yourself again. You are lost. That, which I just explained, is what 'found' looks like.

Don't Forget to Play

There is also a time for levity. Amidst the intense seriousness of my past few weeks, I have generally forgotten about not taking myself too seriously. Life is short, and while this period is critical to my future, it shouldn't be without some lighthearted spirit sprinkled in for good measure from time to time. I was speaking with a good friend the other day and he talked about what it is like for a grown man to return to his boyish spirit. The idea is to maintain elements like playfulness, spontaneity, creativity, and laughter in one's life on a consistent basis. Consider this as the best homework assignment that you will get in a while. You need to know when to stop taking yourself so seriously. You need to learn to let go once in a while and just laugh at how crazy and surreal your situation is and realize that one day in the future this will look so different to you than it does right now.

Call it perspective or context if you wish. Right now, both you and I are lacking the framework to be able to properly contextualize this passage within a greater life path. Since we don't know what follows, it is challenging to have it make sense in the wider angle of your life, the 'zoom-out' so-to-say. So go do something silly. Watch a stand-up comedian on YouTube or Netflix. Play with a baby. Get your hands on a coloring book and lose yourself for an hour or two. In an alone moment, put on some cheerful music that you enjoy and sing and dance around your place. Make farting noises. Do anything that lets your mind have a hard earned rest. You deserve it, and you have worked for it, if only for having read this far in the book. I can be overwhelming when I communicate, I know. I also know that this is a lot of information to handle and digest.

Give yourself some time. Reward yourself with a dose of lightheartedness.

From what I have learned recently, there is no correct path through these situations. There isn't one, unique way of navigating through the darkness. It isn't a one size fits all sort of thing. That's why I insisted earlier in the book that you test these ideas out in your own life. Be willing to do a bit of trial and error with the concepts and suggestions. That way you can see what is and is not a proper fit for your specific circumstances. I just want to help out here. I want to make this easier for you as far as the pain is concerned, and also provide some useful tools for going forward and getting up after you have fallen on your ass so dramatically.

Many people have told me over the years that pretty much all learning and growth comes via suffering and pain. I have heard theories about how love is the way that we get lured into the growth necessary to be stronger and more capable in this life. What I have most definitely noticed in my own life is that my best efforts usually come when my back is against the wall or my butt is on the ground because I fell down doing something wrong. We human beings don't tend to try very hard to improve upon ourselves when everything feels nice and we are happy. That's unfortunate. As a result, the subsequent life challenges are more abrupt and disruptive in nature, often shattering our happiness bubbles as they usher in new learning and wisdom.

I mention this because perhaps you are not really aware of the opportunity here. Life has cracked you open, and like that Leonard Cohen quote that I mentioned, that's exactly where the light gets in. The moment that the pain subsides and the happiness returns, you may very well be far less enthusiastic to reflect upon yourself and do the deep work required to grow. This is not a certainty, but after such a low low, you may find yourself unwilling to engage pain with the same openness and drive that you are experiencing here and now. It's because you need to do it now if you want things to change. You find yourself at a life impasse, one that demands that you do things differently in order to receive a distinct outcome to the one that you are experiencing now. And that's why you are reading this book, isn't it? You want out, out of the crappy pattern, out of the self-defeating mentality, out of the roller coaster of emotions that comes from not being yourself and expressing yourself fully and healthily. You want to learn to listen and hear your partner, and you want them to feel respected, understood, and that they matter very much to you. For whatever reason, that probably was **not** the case in your recent story with them. None of it was, I suspect.

I realize that I don't need to get this perfect, and that nobody gets life perfect. I try to have patience with myself as I take on the gargantuan task of addressing that which I want to work on in my life. I try to maintain a modicum of grace and to be honest with myself as to how long that I am willing to do this work. I am aware that many things will take a long time, perhaps years. I am also aware that all of those paths start with one step, then another, and then another. To walk a thousand miles, you must put one foot in front of the other, over and over again. It may sound cliché, but it is certainly true.

I enjoy walking, and also enjoy running. Sometimes, when I do it in the mornings, I have these little instants during the first ten or fifteen minutes where I psych myself out regarding how far I have left to go before I am done. Many days I thoroughly enjoy myself, but of course there are days where it seems more like work and necessitates more active discipline on my part. I have found that sometimes I just need to allow time to do its thing, to carry me across the divide of desperation or tiredness or unwillingness. It is similar to the phenomenon of procrastination. One of the tried and proven methods to combat procrastination is what is called The Pomodoro Technique. In short, in involves setting a timer and working hard for about 25 minutes. During that time, you just work and nothing else. Afterward you can take a break and distract yourself. Not too long after the rest, you do it all over again. After a few waves, the procrastination tends to morph into a healthy work ethic and enthusiasm for the task. Some days, it is what it takes to make it through.

Sometimes I just need to hang on and survive the lags in power and motivation. They happen. I am sure that they happen to you too, maybe even more than they happen to me. We are all subject to it - nobody has tons of energy all the time. But I assure you that a gentle combination of drive and patience will take you through to the other side of this test, and that you'll look back with a great sense of pride and wonder at what you have achieved by yourself and for yourself. There isn't any turning back once you have established some of these changes, since you will enjoy being different and acting differently.

Boundaries

My wife has had challenges with establishing proper boundaries. Not only with me, but with her family as well. It has proven to be an extremely tough thing for her to learn and implement as quickly and efficiently as she would like. After many years of doing something in a way that doesn't serve you, changes are work intensive to put into play and keep there as concrete, permanent shifts. But with something like boundaries, which by the way is a very relevant subject and in a moment I will delve deeper into it, once you taste the 'new' way of being – you can't ever turn back.

Some of the shifts and alterations that you will engage and apply in your life and in your relationships will have dramatic consequences. In the case of boundaries, if you weren't good at either establishing them or recognizing them, the transformation will probably blow your mind. I know, sounds like an exaggeration, but it isn't.

First let's look at what has been my own personal issue for many years – that of respecting the boundaries of those around me. What does this look like? Hmmm. Interrupting people before they finish their thoughts, holding the belief that somehow my point of view is superior than those of the people around me, an unwillingness to properly listen and understand the ideas being spoken to me, waiting for my turn to talk instead of listening to the person in front of me while they speak, a lack of clarity as to what they are saying or believing because I get stuck in my own thoughts, a rush to finish conversations and to 'get to the point' or conclusion, raising my voice, bullying, controlling, a lack of patience with others but feeling insulted when they fail to be patient with me. Stuff like that. Yup, that's a lot of stuff to have to work on, **I know!** My own personal history and upbringing formed these unhealthy behavior patterns. But I am not restricted to them if I don't want to be, and **of course I don't want to be!** So I have begun to watch myself closely, to note when I slip up, as well as why I do what I do. Some of this stuff requires tons of time and self-observation, free of judgment. If you fail to implement the safety measure of not criticizing yourself too much while you do this, you will be doing the equivalent of stabbing yourself in the chest with a knife over and over. In that case, all the advance will be offset by the lack of self-esteem and appreciation of your own worth as a human being. I know, I know, this is hard. Life is going to be this way at times, just flow with it and the tricky spots will pass, they all do. Just don't give up and you'll eventually begin to feel more free and have more facility of movement.

Now let's take a look at what happens when I start to loosen up some of these behaviors and begin to act in a new way. Afterward, I will explore the opposite behavior pattern, that of my wife, where the lack of these elements creates a totally distinct and problematic scenario for her and those around her. But first let's explore my issues. My tendency to lack respect for the boundaries of others makes me want to be everywhere at once. I often overstep my boundaries and try to do everything for everybody. I become locked into the perception that my way is the only way and that everyone else just has to figure that out and learn to accommodate my method of doing things. Exhausting. So what occurs when I back off?

When I begin to listen instead of chattering so much in my mind, I relax the train's momentum in my head. The gears loosen up and the possibility of not being 'right' creeps into the picture. I begin to ponder points of view that are not my own. I begin to consider alternatives, and lose my hurry for resolution. I start to realize that my goal is a healthy resolution for all parties involved, and not some sort of personal victory. The world of control melts within me and what appears in its place is spacious and relaxing, open and free. I liberate myself from my mental confines and am able to finally enjoy the world around me in a more robust and constructive fashion. The people with whom I am interacting feel honored and respected by my attention which suddenly becomes more active and generous toward them. I empower them to help both me and them here and now. I release my tentacles of control which I had placed on everything and everyone and they get to breathe a sigh of relief and be able to enjoy, once again, their dialogue with me. I stop smothering and dominating the conversations. I stop thinking that I am more important, and more relevant than they are. I begin to humble myself, to leave my ego, and I open myself up to learning from them. **So much better!**

Now let's look at my wife's issues regarding boundaries. Not surprisingly, she falls on the other side of the fence from me. And that made for some catastrophic interactions in the past, especially since we weren't very educated in these matters and we both took **everything** so damn personally. She went the other way. What does that look like? Almost never saying 'no' to me (or other people for that matter), never putting her own well-being above that of the people around her, engaging in self-sacrificing behavior, feeling unable to express all her feelings, not standing up for herself, feeling obligated to serve the happiness of others, not marking her limits, not letting people know when they are crossing lines with her, not letting people know when they are mistreating her or disrespecting her, not being assertive, choosing peace over disagreements, not wanting to rock the boat, constant feeling of compromise (which in turn creates an underlying resentment), and never seeming to have time just for herself. Also just as exhausting as my list, right?

Just like I did with my list, let's take a look at what happens when she begins to speak up for herself and make herself a key priority in her actions. Initially, people around her may be offended or surprised to have her draw lines and defend them. That's perfectly normal. But what follows soon after is a great respect that everyone develops for her. If a person respects themselves, others will follow suit. People begin to better understand their place and role within their interactions, they subsequently back off, and they exhibit respect toward the will and choices of the person. In my wife's case, all of a sudden she is empowered and returns to having control over her relationships. A person without clear boundaries has everyone meddling and telling them what to do and how to do it and when. Once they stand upright and return that energy inward to themselves (which had prior been projected outward), their world changes. They get free time, they get their own word back in discussions and disagreements, and they become less willing to compromise and more willing to take care of themselves. People stop being abusive, rude, stop interrupting them, and stop crossing lines with the person. This allows the freshly empowered person to take back that which they mistakenly gave away long ago.

Interesting, right? In both cases, it is a misallocation of power than needs to be recalibrated and rebalanced. In both cases, both the person and those with whom they relate are uncomfortable and out of place, as such the interactions involve much suffering and frustration on all sides. If I am bossy or pushy, people will be rejected by my behavior and avoid me. If I am the opposite, and let everyone push me around, then I will be unhappy and I will ultimately resent them (and myself for having allowed the scenario to flourish).

Boundaries are an essential part of communication, since they allow both parties inside of a relationship to feel safe and empowered. If these things are absent, then the communication begins to break down and both people end up finding themselves in positions that don't correspond to them. As such, the relationship begins to incorporate unstable aspects. People need to be free to express themselves, to be heard, for their opinions and feelings to be welcomed, and for the relationship to hold space for them. This, of course, must include things that are uncomfortable and complicated – in fact, that's the part where this strength is most handy. If the communication is out of kilter, imbalanced and such, then when things get challenging the situation becomes increasingly uncomfortable. The mild incongruences and compromises are accentuated. Both sides inevitably get squeezed and forced to inhabit spaces that are inappropriate and damaging (to both people). At its core, it is about feeling safe to be yourself and not about being asked (or worse, obligated) to be someone or something else.

The quicker that you can comprehend and adjust to this idea, the better that you will feel. Like I mentioned before, some things have an almost immediate impact and the consequences are felt right away. This is one of those things. With just a slow and methodical effort on your part, you can create tremendous space and flexibility in your relationship. And with a partner who has gone away, this means that you can breathe easier and they feel less threatened and pushed away. This is excellent for both of you at this time.

Mirrors

I have often been forced to deal with my pride over these past few weeks. Sometimes it is an unwillingness on my part to admit mistakes. Sometimes it is when I find myself tending toward my old habits and not wanting to listen. Sometimes I am just angry at my spouse for having left. And all of this is fine, since I cannot be expected to just wake up one morning and be a totally new man. But I allow for these feelings and for these struggles of my own ego against my world - against my current and novel choices. If I don't let these things come up inside of me and I don't give them a voice, then I begin a path of resentment against myself, and that's just a trap. I see it as a kind of pushing forward, then letting go, then pushing a bit in a different way, then letting go. It is like a gentle coaxing of myself by myself toward a new way of being. If I push too hard, then I end up with an inner fight. If I don't push enough, then I don't move. Just like I have been doing, you will need to find that sweet spot where things can shift at the speed that they should without making it unreasonable and/or unsustainable. Time will teach you this - time and effort. Luckily for you, you are here on your own with a good dose of time available to you to figure this stuff out. Well, you have me with you, and as I said before I sincerely hope that my words provide solace for you within your experience.

In my life, I have found that two relationships thus far have proven the most rewarding and challenging simultaneously. The first is my marriage to my wife and the second is my relationship with my son. I have found that when another human being shares such close confines with me, and does so for extended periods of time, that tons of things come up for me. I get triggered, I have many behaviors mirrored back at me, and I get confronted regularly. It is hard to have a sense of objectivity in these relationships and I am dependent to a great degree on them to tell me what their experience is in order to successfully navigate territory in conjunction with them. For the sake of this text, I have focused mostly on the relationship of my marriage because it is more central to the theme. Of course, as I heal and transform one aspect of my life, other parts adjust as well. I am shifting the nature of how I engage my external environment.

My wife has been near me or next to me for many years now. Her perspective on me never ceases to amaze me. Sometimes she can tell what I am going through by noticing a subtle curling of the corner of my mouth or a movement in my cheeks, or the shift in my gaze. She also seems capable of misinterpreting my very basic communications. Isn't that just nuts? The closeness muffles our clarity sometimes I suppose. But I have never in my life had someone know so much about me. When I really take a moment to ponder the depth of her knowledge and wisdom about me, I realize how astounding it really is. This means that she knows all my demons as well as all my most beautiful and kind features. She has insights into my fears, my worries, my grandest aspirations and my dreams. So here, in honor of the gift of self-knowledge that she provides for me, I am going to talk about appreciation and gratitude.

You may not be feeling it very much these days, because it may be mixed up with resentment and anger and loneliness and sadness, but surely somewhere inside of you, kicking around, is your appreciation for your partner. It's time here to delve into that.

Allow your mind to travel outside of yourself, and into the realm of your loved one. Look at her or him, slowly and methodically evaluating and noticing the details of their physical form. Try and see as much texture and detail as possible - go into all the nooks and crannies of their body. Pay attention to their smell. Look into their eyes. What color is their hair? How do they like to have their hair? How do you prefer it? Are their hands big? Soft? Do they have wrinkles around their eyes? What color are their eyes? Is their skin smooth? Which areas of their body do you enjoy more and which ones less. Try to really explore here, to feel it all, and to allow your senses to fully take in their person. Do you feel like you can easily do this? Or are they a bit faded in your mind? What about their voice, how does it resonate for you to imagine hearing them speaking to you? Be gentle here, the exercise is just one of observation and experience, so if you find yourself getting overly emotional then maybe pull back a tiny bit and try it again another time.

Create a mental panorama that is completely filled to the brim with the characteristics of your partner. The good stuff **and** the bad stuff, or at least what you consider those things to be from your point of view (be willing to question the qualifiers that you place upon their traits from time to time since it is healthy to do so). What are the nuances of how they look at you and how they speak to you? What do their eyes do when they are happy? What about when they are supportive? How about when they are crying? When they were deeply in love with you what did you see in their face? Take it all in. Don't lie to yourself as to how much you love them or loved them. It's fine. It's great actually.

Now is not a time to lie. It is not a time to pretend that my or your feelings are not real or existent. To the contrary, I am going to chaperone you right smack dab into the middle of it all, and then drop you off and allow to gaze in awe at the love that you have allowed yourself to have right here in your life. At some point in the process, you will gain the capability to see the distinction between what is inside you and what is outside of you. And this representation of your partner is entirely *inside* of you right now. So let's go on a journey and check it out!

Why do you love them? What are the attributes of their personality that most inspire you? What are the greatest things about them? What are their strengths? What do you most admire about them? What are you most grateful for about them? What are you most thankful for? How have they touched you deeply? Try to remember specific instances of this. What have they taught you? What are they teaching you *right now*?

Thank them. If you believe in God, thank God for them. Right now. Take a second, breathe this all in and out. Fill your entire being with gratitude and appreciation for everything that you have received during your relationship with this person, as well as everything that you are learning and getting from it now in this new phase. Cry if it you want. Be willing to experience the totality of what this individual means to you. Feel your heart swell and hurt if that's what is here. Don't hide from this. There is much to gain from feeling this, in its more pure form, without judgment.

Consider the possibility that your current state and experience may not be exactly what you think that it is. Follow me a bit into this. There may be things here that you are not contemplating. And the fact that they fail to appear in your consciousness doesn't mean that they are not there. There is a very wide array of things in front of you right now. Something incredible lies square behind this idea for you. It is just below the surface. It is so easy to get caught in one way of seeing things, or one way of thinking about things. I do it all the time. But ease out of that for a sec. Give yourself the opportunity to be a bit more than you are, to see beyond your scope, out over the horizon and into the unknown.

Also, consider the idea that your partner is not in your life to serve the purpose that you have had in your mind all this time. There is so much more to life than what we limit our sights on. My wife means the world to me. These days I am only beginning to truly value the vastness of what she is providing me. And this includes her recent choice to leave me. In my life, I don't think that I have ever grown so quickly and willingly. I cannot deny this truth. I am empowered as a result of her choice. Not because of her, but because of me. But she showed me the door. And I chose to open it and walk through it.

Owning It With Gratitude

This is the part of the book where you say thanks. You get to be thankful for everything, and for everyone who has brought you to a deeper understanding of who you are and who you want to be. Spend plenty of time on this, since it will soften and heal your insides. Nobody ever got sick from feeling an overabundance of gratitude. Revel in what you have here and now. See it. Feel it. Immerse yourself in whatever you can see and perceive of your own personal bounty in this moment in time and space. Don't worry, I'll let you get back to mourning if you so wish in just a moment. If you insist, you can be anywhere you want to be in yourself. If you only take away one thing from this book, let it be that you are the master of your own internal domain. Where your awareness and consciousness **is,** that's where you **are**. Where you direct your focus is where you will be, whether it be inside of aspects of your reality that serve you, or others that make you suffer and feel bad. Of course, external circumstances and forces will always be at play in your world, but you'd be surprised to truly comprehend how little that has to do with your overall experience. It is shocking really once you really begin to explore the depths of your own control of the story. Consider the flavors, the colors, the sensations, the tone and perspective that everything has. So much of this is formed inside of your head and heart.

I am responsible for my world right now. At the end of the day, I must answer to myself for what is going on and how I choose to react to it. How do I want to feel? What am I willing to learn? To change? To work on? To see? To admit to? To recognize and accept? These are big questions. Courage is underrated when it comes to this stuff. Be courageous! Be daring! Begin to appreciate anxious fear as a reliable sign that something may in fact be worth doing. What was scary and intimidating as a child may be useful to you now, and you may need to update your own internal systems to welcome the possibilities of doing things in a distinct manner than you did ages ago. I have learned that my own systems need regular maintenance. I constantly need to reevaluate what is good for me and what is not. Who is good for me, and who is not. What makes me feel good and what doesn't. Which actions represent compromise and self-depreciation and which represent me growing up and being stronger and wiser?

When we allow our energy to be hijacked by fear, we rob ourselves of both trust and empowerment. It is the same energy. Choose wisely.

I have just today encountered a new pearl of wisdom. I wrote it out, then read it and re-read it until it sat long enough in my mind for me to capture some of its essence. I recommend that you do the same. Allow me to elaborate on the idea and perhaps I can present it in a way that makes it clear and applicable for you in your life.

It is so easy for me to fall into a state of fear or preoccupation or worry, or any combination of the three. As I mentioned earlier, I grew up in an environment that didn't imbue me with trust for my world. To the contrary, I developed the belief that those who are closest to me should be distrusted and kept at a safe distance from my heart and person. I developed a sense that fear would always act as a tool to protect me from the pains of this world. In my childhood, my most experienced form of punishment was abandonment. Let me explain that. My parents were most of the time either physically or emotionally unavailable, or both at the same time. That means that when I was sick or felt bad or needed to be hugged or consoled or whatever, it was a challenge (to say the least) to receive anything from them beyond irritation and anger. I grew up believing that

I was a burden to them and that my problems were insignificant and not worthy of my or their attention and love. I am not writing this to elicit your pity or to swamp you in some psycho-babble; I am only giving a bit of context to my history so that you can have a better grasp of where I am coming from when I write.

I wasn't allowed to get sick as a child, and if I felt sick I needed to prove it to my mother. The best example of this that I can give you is when I got intestinal worms. In short, my mother just refused to believe me. So I had to actually show her the proof. Yes, it was horrific! But that was my context, and it gives me insights into the struggles of my recent past and present. Perhaps taking a good look at where you come from and the lessons that you were taught is in order here. Your past is not your future, but it holds many answers regarding your life trajectory. It also can explain the root issues behind your present behaviors.

Getting back to the idea, it could be said that my predisposition has been historically toward a difficulty in trusting those closest to me. This includes me. You see, because I was unable to change these painful scenarios when I was little, I created the belief that not only could I do nothing, but that the person that I loved was incapable as well. Not only that, but that I would be ultimately abandoned when I most needed love. What a terrible thing to hold true. Such a loss!

So how do I work from within this situation? Well, the fear tends to just barge right in a hijack my energy. Perhaps something goes wrong, or I have a fight or argument with my wife, and suddenly I am afraid that she will leave me as a result. And as fate would have it, I married someone who tends toward running away when things get rough. The combination of our tendencies has made for us pushing each other's fear buttons constantly. I hold tight, she pushes away. Then I hold tighter, and she runs away. Rinse and repeat.

So where's the solution?

First of all, I have worked **a lot** on healing myself on the inside. A lot of crying, a lot of brutal honesty about who I am, where I come from, and why I believe what I believe. The most important element, in my opinion, is recognizing the patterns and reactions that we have to what is happening around us. This includes what we do, when we do it, and how we do it. With that information, I enable and empower myself to begin to see what I am doing wrong and really get a good grasp on how the mechanism functions. I also have had to admit to myself, on a profound level, that many of my past patterns are completely outdated and dysfunctional for my well-being. This is perhaps more subtle than many realize.

We do what we do because on some level not only is it what we know, but it is what **we believe will work best for us**. Read that again. We, as human beings, operate in a way that internally seems to be the best way to do things. Often this is merely the case because we only **know one way to do things**. Maybe read that again too. I cannot emphasize enough the power of these ideas. So, even if our methods consistently put us in compromised and weak positions with respect to what our truly desired outcome is, we continue to do them since our mind tells us that it is our best option each time that a problem arises. It reminds me of the saying that if all we have is a hammer then every problem starts to look like a nail.

OK, so the first step is to bring as much awareness and consciousness to the problem, and to explore what **our role** is in how the problems develop and how they are handled by us. Don't even concern yourself with your partner just yet here. We'll get to that in a bit.

Now, watch what happens when our resources get hijacked by our past. And our past, if it was a rough one, especially in matters of love (which is probably the case in close to 100% of the people reading this book), will be represented energetically by fear. Perhaps it is the fear of this relationship not working out, or fear that our partner will break our heart, or fear that our partner will abandon us (which they just did, so there is that prophecy fulfilled). Maybe it is the fear that we will fail in our quest to be the man or woman that we want to be. It could be the fear that we will fail in our career. I often fear that I will be a bad parent, or a bad spouse. I sometimes fear that my partner will cheat on me, or that my partner will fall out of love with me. Maybe you fear that your partner doesn't find you attractive, or that they are bored of you. There are a plethora of fears that could come into play here. Fear can come in all shapes and sizes.

Now check out what happens once the fear rolls in. It steals the same energy that you have available to do two other things: firstly to trust in your partner to be strong and dependable as a supportive and loving element in the relationship, and second your own empowered ability to take care of yourself within the relationship and subsequently to be a powerful force in securing love and strength internally and externally. Sorry if that was a big mouthful, but I needed to make sure that it was properly stated so as not to dilute it or diminish it. Take a few moments to re-read it and let it sink in.

If you are operating from a source of fear, you cannot be trusting of your partner in that moment. Not deeply at least. And if you are coming from a place of fear, you cannot be empowered within yourself. Not profoundly. Do you see it yet? There is an internal choice, one that we all need to be made aware of; of an allocation of energy resources that doesn't serve us or our relationships. We hinder ourselves and weaken our bond with our mate. We debilitate everyone involved and make them feel very small and helpless. And it very much does **not** need to be the case. All that you have to do is feed the other side of the equation.

Work on trusting your partner with all your heart. Learn their strengths. Appreciate and be grateful for their personal power, their resourcefulness, their creativity, and their spontaneity. Work on realizing that they are just as much a participant in the relationship as you are, and as such deserve equal footing and standing in the power structure. Try making a list of the characteristics of their personality that best exemplify their creativity and spontaneity and resourcefulness. Have you been appreciative of these things or have you taken them for granted? I took my wife for granted, and only now am I beginning to see the scope of it and how it felt for her. A fully empowered partner will probably not run away. In fact, they will likely seek out the space next to you since it will feel liberating and enjoyable. Everyone wants to feel free and safe to be themselves, and this is an essential part of you learning how to provide that for your partner.

Also, work on developing your own strength. Develop and nourish trust in yourself. Bring your awareness to the fact that you can change your life scenarios if you apply your will with wisdom. I invite you to know what you **can** do and what you **can** begin practicing - all the time. How do you begin to do this? Try changing things when you feel bad. Each time that you can remember to do so, when you find yourself feeling bad, I want you to try to change something very simple. You are going to attempt to change something small. Watch your pattern closely and see which pieces of your puzzle can move around or operate differently. Try changing things when you feel frustrated, and try changing things when life appears difficult or impossible. Don't be a hero, just see if you can do little shifts. Start small, but be consistent. Set the bar low, and check out how many times you can clear it. Educate yourself on your **real** limits and possibilities. You will surely be happily surprised to understand just how much you genuinely can change all by yourself. This book and your efforts right now are a testament to that. This is the meat of the matter – the hard part.

What you will notice, and what has become crystal clear to me on this very morning writing this, is that it is almost always one or the other, either fear or trust and empowerment. It is never both, at least not to great degrees. So not only do fear, worry, and preoccupation weaken both you and your partner as well as your relationship, but **they remove the tools necessary to make everything better, stronger, more stable, and reliable**. Interesting, isn't it? Pay attention to this and see if it rings true for you. Don't just take my word for it. Look at past scenarios in your relationship, and using this new lens see if they look different. Look at fights and difficult periods. If you can, try and contemplate how your partner saw you and how they saw things in general in those times.

So Where Are We Now?

I am arriving at the end of what I have to share about this subject matter. I by no means expect to have resolved all of my own or your problems, but hopefully the text has been of great assistance in the process. I firmly believe that all of life is a learning process, and that we are constantly refining and improving upon ourselves, and that the journey is one of purifying ourselves from elements that are outdated and destructive. We remove that which we no longer need, and then we replace them with newly learned things that work better for us and make us (and those around us) feel better and live better.

So what do you think? Where is your head at after having almost completed this book? How does your heart feel? If you compare where you are now to where you were when you first picked up the book, are you happy with the difference? If I have done anything at all, I have enabled your direct contact with both of these parts of yourself, which in of itself is a wonderful thing since it keeps you from becoming estranged to your own inner world. In fact, if you can properly tie into these things (more importantly connecting to **how you feel)**, then you can surely make your way from there. You can find your way home, so to speak.

I don't believe that life is black and white, or that there are easily defined answers for issues of the heart. I think that there are definitely times where the direction and path is crystal clear, but unfortunately for all of us life is confusing a lot of the time. **Sometimes the very purpose of the path is to help you develop your ability to listen and see clearly what is in front of your eyes and inside your own self**. It would serve you well to concern yourself much less with the desired outcome than with what you need to do here and now. I have found that looking too far ahead often clouds our judgment and clarity in the present moment.

In my personal journey, I even found that there was a moment when both my gut and my heart signaled me to do something that I have stated here is a big no-no. There was a moment wherein I felt that my very limited communication with my wife in the weeks after she left me was not serving me in the way that I needed. In fact, I struggled for a day or two to determine whether or not I wanted to contact her out of sheer desperation or sadness, or if it was because my sparse communication was not being received by her in the way that I intended. I found myself in a tough predicament. I have stated very clearly in this book that if someone runs away and leaves us because we are likely already overwhelming them or that they are feeling overwhelmed by the relationship, that it would only make it worse to chase them. I still agree with this.

Let me tell you what happened, and I will explain why it is that I insisted early on in this text that it should be a process of trial and error. I have been adamant that you try out the ideas and see what works and does not work for you during this time. But keep in mind that I am mentioning this at the end of this book because the stuff that comes prior is the base from which you can begin to operate in a more flexible way, and not the other way around. There is a constructive process over the course of this book, one with different goals and methods to be applied in stages. What works at the start could theoretically be obsolete by the end. It is a general map, as opposed to a specific schedule to follow.

I was trying to learn how to be more receptive to my wife's words. This was not a particularly easy task after she had written her eloquent discourse about my personal failures and the failures of our relationship (and sent it to me via email). I kept my communication (via email, since she explicitly asked me not to call her or show up at her mother's home where she was staying in a different city to where our home is located) short and to the point. My intention was that she would feel listened to and respected, that she had my active attention, and that hopefully she would express more of what she had kept bottled up for years. So my replies were to the point and asking for her to speak freely via her words. Unfortunately, there was a bigger gap in between our words than I had imagined.

I took a risk early one morning. Several weeks had already gone by after she had left me, including a fair bit of time with very limited to no communication (limited to emails as I mentioned earlier). I felt in my gut that something was off, that something wasn't lining up properly. I considered calling her sister. Now, I'd like for you to understand that such an act comes with some very real and serious potentially damaging consequences. There was a possibility that her sister would not want to speak with me. There was a possibility that my wife would be even more pissed off with me since I went behind her back to ask her sister about her. There was a possibility that her sister would ask me to never call again and that I leave her alone and not involve her. In short, I had a real chance of making things much worse for myself. But in my gut, a voice was speaking loud and clear - so I made the telephone call.

I ended up speaking with my wife's sister for over an hour. The most important detail that I got from the conversation was that my wife had completely missed the intended point of how and why my communication with her had been so curt and without my own expression of my sentiments.

In fact, my wife had considered only two potential reasons as to why I was acting so 'strangely' toward her in my short replies: one, that she had actually made me crazy in breaking up with me (that I was no longer rational), and two, that I was mocking her. Mocking her! I was in shock when her sister said that to me. It couldn't be further from the truth. I asked her sister to speak to her and mention where I was coming from and I sat down to write my wife a letter.

I wrote a page explaining my actions, sharing my feelings, and talking about my pain and my process. And with the risk of overwhelming an already overwhelmed woman, I sent it out and prayed for the best. Her reply came within minutes. She told me how comforting it was to hear how I felt, and that she felt as if she was being vulnerable in telling me how she felt and couldn't understand why I wasn't doing the same. She was relieved to hear that I was also struggling and that I, personally, wasn't seeking a divorce from her (even though she clearly said in her letter that she was seeking a divorce from me – which goes to show how intense emotions can take over and dominate the horizon of one's sight). She also said that on one hand she wanted to hear my voice, but on the other hand she felt fear and hate towards me.

I took another risk. I called her. Of course as luck would have it, her mother picked up the phone and I ended up speaking for a half an hour with her first. But then I spoke with my wife for several hours. I eventually ended up having a Skype video call with her, for many more hours. And thus began a process of thawing the ice between us.

The point is this: I broke a rule that I had held to be a golden rule of how to act. This is precisely why I insist that none of this is black and white. But you must **first** appreciate **why** the space and silence is needed. Only **then** can you begin to see when and where to be flexible and accommodating to your specific reality. This isn't easy, it isn't meant to be. Transformation and growth takes work, lots of work, and time.

Consider this: If I had not developed my own sense of worth and self-preservation, returning my attention toward a state of self-respect, then I would not have been able to connect with my wife from a place of personal power. That's why I needed to be in a state of essentially very limited contact for an extended period of time. Only you, in your most honest place within yourself, can know where you are and what you are ready to do. Also, if I had attempted to contact her prior to that particular day, she would have probably been too filled with hate and animosity to have been capable of receiving me in a healthy way. It would have been counter-productive for both of us, and I would have pushed our connection further away for an even longer period of time. I would have also potentially damaged the chances of it ever even happening that she would be interested in contact with me.

Please understand that there is no certain outcome. Ever. There is no forever, or happily ever after. That only exists in fairy tales. Reality is different; it is messier and more requiring of your constant investment and participation. If you want to be in a sustainable relationship, then you ought to be willing to remember the place that you were in at the start of your relationship (when you were trying to win him or her over). You need to make them feel wonderful and beautiful and sought after (all over again). Because that's exactly how everyone wants to feel. That should never be forgotten or under-valued. I sincerely believe that without a consistent push forward into love and dedication, **all the time**, that a sort of decay begins to set in and couples begin a slow spiral downward. Like I have said earlier in the book, your partner wants to see you embodying your best effort, living completely, in a satisfied and passionate way. It needs to be both obvious and visible.

They want you to be moving forward and chasing your dreams, seeking out your personal fulfillment. Who wouldn't want to accompany someone like that? People like that are magnetic, attractive, powerful, and they have an aura of leadership and freshness. Imagine going to a grocery store and looking at the produce. Are you going to pick the stuff that looks fresh and alive, or the stuff that has already begun to rot and will go off sooner? Relationships function in a similar fashion. Life attracts life.

Your partner will light up from your desire to see them happy and free. Make it your life goal to give that to yourself as well, and to provide the inspiration for anyone and everyone who comes into contact with you. Have everyone you meet leave the experience feeling closer to these feelings of inspiration and vitality.

I think that life itself responds proportionately to the personal investment of time and effort that you put into it. If you profoundly want to change certain aspects of yourself, and if you wish to fight for your relationship, then throw yourself into the work and just push forward. The rest will fall into place (as it should). Just don't forget what I said just now, that there are no guaranteed outcomes in life. Even the best laid plans, as Steinbeck said in his novel Of Mice and Men, often go awry, meaning that they end up somewhere quite different to where we intended.

Final Notes

Be willing to try and fail. Be willing to put it all on the line. None of us will make it out of this life alive - that being the one real certainty in this existence. There is nothing quite as annoying and haunting as the remorse of not having done something when your inclination and your heart have clearly pushed you in a particular direction. There is something so beautiful about a man or a woman who is not afraid to make a fool of themselves in a brave expression of love. Once you get past that first moment of apprehension, and you propel yourself into action, then you'll discover that life begins to bloom and surprise. Your attitude toward the crossing the precipice from the known into the void of the unknown must be one of courage and determination.

There is a magic place that exists in between an idea and the action fulfilling and enacting said idea in the real world. It is where leaders and heroes are formed. Usually it only requires a moment of intention, of pure motivation, to go forward and 'see what happens' if you do something. Most people cower from this challenge and prefer to stay inside a realm of perceived safety. What is often referred to as a person's comfort zone is the area of supposed safety. This is where a person will repeat familiar patterns and habits because they tend towards more predictable outcomes. **Nothing exciting or visceral happens here**. It is a sort of dead space, where relationships and people go to stagnate and decay. My goal with this book is to gently at times, and not so gently in other instances, move you the reader toward the scarier and less predictable place – the '*I don't know what will happen if I do this*' place. Over and over again. The purpose of the exercise is to familiarize you with the notion and action of acting **from** a place of true purpose, as opposed to acting with a desired end result in mind. Is this clear? The focus needs to be on where you are coming from, the purity so to speak of your drive forward when you choose a path. We need to have all our attention on the starting point and lose interest and obsession about the ending point.

If you genuinely want a life that feels better, one where you feel more like yourself (especially the parts of yourself that are the most fun to experience), then you need to be willing to go places that are more daunting and challenging. You must extend beyond your current limitations. This needs to become your norm. It isn't easy. I am not going to sugarcoat this. You will have to push your limits.

I lived forty years on this earth with an obsessive impulse toward controlling my circumstances as well as the outcomes of my choices. It has often driven me toward painful scenarios that have once and again shown me the same lessons. The principal lesson being that I need to let go more often. I have learned that I need to be able to take risks and slowly begin to play with the idea of enjoying the mystery of life. When I was little, I marveled at how amazing life was. An example of this is how I would get excited and thrilled when I would be inside an airplane that was taking off. The rush, the sounds, the atmosphere of anticipation of moments that were just about to happen - all these things filled me with an abundance of life. My disposition was toward hurling myself into the unknown and enjoying as much of it as I could. Somewhere in my later 20s and early 30s, I began to feel my mortality much more. I began to worry about my future, my finances, my responsibilities, etc. I slowly embarked upon a journey of favoring safer alternatives, and of choosing comfort and routine over adventure. I could see it in how I managed my home, and how I would eventually bring up my son. I could see it in my relationships, and my tendency to attempt to control my partner. For my wife, this part of me was experienced by her as asphyxiating, giving her claustrophobia and an impetus to leave and run away. Of course it did, it is all so clear in retrospect. But it took her leaving me for me to really see these things clearly. It took being alone and reflecting upon my life choices and attitude to be able to properly assess and evaluate how I was living my life and how much it truly contrasted with how I needed to live my life in order to be happy.

I have a great exercise for you to do now. Get yourself a few pieces of paper and something to write with. This exercise will serve to highlight the important differences between how you currently live your life and how you would likely be much more satisfied living your life if you made a few changes. On your first piece of paper, I would like to ask you to make a list of the things that you don't like about yourself and your life right now. Try to be honest, but not cruel. Resist the temptation to beat yourself up here. Include the reasons which fall under your umbrella of accountability for why your partner left you. Be as specific and detailed as you can. Take your time and be meticulous.

Rest for a few moments. Breathe. If you went deep enough, there will be a lot of powerful feelings that have come to the surface. Allow them. Flow with them. Do your very best to withhold judgment.

Next, I would like you to try and see if you can identify the behavior patterns and choices that you have made or have been making that led to many of these situations and traits that you don't particularly like or want to remain in your life. Avoid answers like "I am stupid" or "I make poor choices" or anything that isn't really a tangible thing that can be worked with. In short, avoid negative generalizations about yourself, because it makes it harder to do anything about it. Try to identify specific comments that you make or have made, or gestures, or your most obvious reactions in tense and conflictive scenarios. Play out past conversations and fights in your head, but stay clearly focused upon how you act from your side of things. Go as deep as you are comfortable exploring.

Take a few moments to be where you are. This is not an easy exercise.

Now, take a new piece of paper and make a list of how you want to feel. How do you want your life to look? Who is in it? Who is close to you? How do you act? What scenarios are most desirable? What does your attitude look like? How about your confidence? Your self-respect? Your optimism about your success? Again, be as detailed as you can be. With all of the new tools that you have acquired over the course of reading this book, this exercise should now be more revealing and useful for you.

We have now arrived at the best part. With the most sincerity and wisdom possible, and using your best judgment and clarity, I want you to go through this new list and try and come up with the choices and behaviors that will lead you toward it. Each detail. Each feeling. Work individually with everything and see if you can find out, for yourself, within yourself, how you can get there. Just like I mentioned beforehand, avoid sweeping generalizations. Go line by line. Take all the time in the world. Just make sure to arrive at your answers, the ones that have the most resonance for you.

What I suspect that you will encounter via this process is the fact that the way that you do things or have done things in the past do not bring you closer to where you want to be. This may seem obvious but there is an underlying power to be found here – specifically the power to change yourself for the better. As you hone in on the particular things that you do out of habit instead of out of a desire to feel better, you provide yourself with the choice to act differently. **This is where you want to be**. This is where you make subtle and definitive shifts that change everything. All that remains is the discipline and consistency to repeat the actions until they are new habits. **It isn't enough to want to change and to get something right once**. In part, there is a success worth being proud of if you achieve something, even just once, that you were unable to do beforehand. What a great feeling it is to try something new and to be rewarded with a totally new outcome – a more desired outcome that is better for you! It is great, but if you want more, and I would like to believe that at this point in the book that you do really want something greater, then you need to get your hands dirty and to do these things time and time again. Act differently, then repeat the action until it sticks.

So, has this book done something for you? Do you feel better? Are you more relaxed and confident regarding your situation? Have you learned to empower yourself? Are you inspired? I know that this place is tricky and painful. Life oftentimes puts us in places where nothing is very clear and everything hurts. I feel for you. I really do. My heart goes out to you. Being left is a terrible thing, at least until you really turn it around and make it work for you. And if you can do this here and now, then imagine what you will be able to do in other areas of your life when you face challenging situations. These particular lessons are by no means limited to this specific life experience. My wish is that you are able to take some of these little pearls of wisdom and run with them. Hopefully they are like seeds that grow into plants and bear wonderful fruit for you. I would love to know that my efforts have resulted in a better life for you. I would love to know that my words have taught you to care for yourself better. I am in this life with you, and in this hardship with you, and I have to say that I am appreciative of what I have learned and discovered through writing this book. It has been a personal therapy for me, a sort of consultation process with the wisest parts of my being. It has been my seeking truth and power from within me, for me and for you. I have given from the best part of me in this book, and I really hope that it has made all the difference in the world for you in your life journey. I wish you success and joy. May your heart take solace from the recent pain, and may it open and shine for the entire world to see. Be well.

It makes me very happy that you have made it all the way through to the end of the book. I sincerely hope from the bottom of my heart that my words and ideas have been a valuable resource for you in your journey through your hardship. I put my heart and soul into this book, with the desire that people could be more empowered within themselves.

I'd like to ask a favor of you. Please write a review for the book. If my book was helpful to you, it will probably be equally as helpful for others, and they will only know that if you are kind enough to share a few words. I would be very appreciative of the gesture.

I wrote a novel, called Adam (The Story of a Man to Be), and I would love for you to read it. Here it is:
https://www.amazon.com/gp/product/B078H2JHV9/

I would like to invite you to follow me on my Facebook author page, so that you can keep abreast with my most recent ideas and projects.
https://www.facebook.com/MichaelEliVineberg/

You can also find me on Twitter at this link:
https://twitter.com/M_Vineberg

My YouTube channel is at this link:
https://www.youtube.com/channel/UCAht398fqE66x0QldOZL9hw

Also, please check out my other two non-fiction books.

I'm Human, Now What? (Semi-Precious Thoughts on Life)
https://www.amazon.com/gp/product/B01MU8XBV8/

The Love Metric
https://www.amazon.com/gp/product/B071VRTMTT/

87542475R00057

Made in the USA
Lexington, KY
26 April 2018